The Upside Down, Backward Life Of Disciples

Cycle C Sermons for Proper 17 — Thanksgiving Based on the Gospel Lessons

Jill J. Duffield

CSS Publishing Company, Inc.
Lima, Ohio

THE UPSIDE DOWN, BACKWARDS LIFE OF DISCIPLES

FIRST EDITION
Copyright © 2021
by CSS Publishing Co., Inc.

The original purchaser may print and photocopy material in this publication for use as it was intended (worship material for worship use; educational material for classroom use; dramatic material for staging or production). No additional permission is required from the publisher for such copying by the original purchaser only. Inquiries should be addressed to: Permissions, CSS Publishing Company, Inc., 5450 N. Dixie Highway, Lima, Ohio 45807.

Library of Congress Cataloging-in-Publication Data

Names: Duffield, Jill J., author. Title: The upside down, backwards life of disciples : Cycle C sermons for Proper 17 - Thanksgiving based on the Gospel lessons / Jill J. Duffield. Description: First edition. | Lima, Ohio : CSS Publishing Company, Inc., [2021] Identifiers: LCCN 2021013908 | ISBN 9780788030284 | ISBN 9780788030291 (ebook) Subjects: LCSH: Bible. Luke--Sermons. | Common lectionary (1992). Year C. | Church year sermons. Classification: LCC BS2595.54 .D84 2021 | DDC 252.6--dc23 LC record available at https://lccn.loc.gov/2021013908

For more information about CSS Publishing Company resources, visit our website at www.csspub.com, email us at csr@csspub.com, or call (800) 241-4056.

e-book:
ISBN-13: 978-0-7880-3029-1
ISBN-10: 0-7880-3029-9

ISBN-13: 978-0-7880-3028-4
ISBN-10: 0-7880-3028-0   ELECTRONICALLY PRINTED

For Joseph, Jessie, and Marissa
with love and gratitude for all the sermons you endured.

Contents

A Place At The Table — 7
Proper 17 / Ordinary Time 22
Luke 14:1, 7-14

Calculated Christianity — 12
Proper 18 / Ordinary Time 23
Luke 14:25-33

Where's The One? — 17
Proper 19 / Ordinary Time 24
Luke 15:1-10

Give Me Your Word — 21
Proper 20 / Ordinary Time 25
Luke 16:1-13

The Great Divide — 27
Proper 21 / Ordinary Time 26
Luke 16:19-31

Upside Down And Backward — 31
Proper 22 / Ordinary Time 27
Luke 17:5-10

The Power Of Proximity — 35
Proper 23 / Ordinary Time 28
Luke 17:11-19

Persistent Prayer — 40
Proper 24 / Ordinary Time 29
Luke 18:1-8

Don't Hold Back — 45
Proper 25 / Ordinary Time 30
Luke 18:9-14

Chief Among Sinners   *50*
Proper 26 / Ordinary Time 31
Luke 19:1-10

For All The Saints   *55*
All Saints' Day
Luke 6:20-31

The God of Abraham, Isaac, and Jacob   *60*
Proper 27 / Ordinary Time 32
Luke 20:27-38

Bear Witness   *65*
Proper 28 / Ordinary Time 33
Luke 21:5-19

IF You Are The Christ...   *68*
Proper 29 / Ordinary Time 34
Luke 23:33-43

Contraband Communion   *72*
Thanksgiving Day
John 6:25-35

Proper 17 / Ordinary Time 22
Luke 14:1, 7-14

A Place At The Table

Preacher's kids, PKs for short, know a lot about church. Earlier this year, I was given the best church tour of my life by a young PK. I was in a town just outside of Atlanta, Georgia, to do a preaching series and the pastor of this church, a colleague and friend for many years, went to check on a worship detail while I waited in his office. As I waited, his eight-year-old daughter seized on the opportunity to show me around. I was escorted by a church expert in a princess costume into Sunday school rooms, through a dimly lit basement hallway, around the office work area, up into the balcony of the sanctuary, shown the small hole through which to peep at the people below, taken across street to the fellowship hall and finally, into the kitchen, where I was told where the cookies were stashed. Not only that, I was informed of when events took place in said spaces: Wednesday night suppers, the pre-school, children's choir practice. Every nook and cranny, every happening and hangout were explained in detail. I loved it. I loved her comfort in the place. I loved her confidence. I loved her sense of ownership and belonging.

She'd been welcomed to congregational spaces from the time of her birth, and nothing was off limits from her exploration: the pulpit, choir loft, her dad's desk chair; all her domain.

Watching her bound through the church, eager to tell me all about not just the space, but the people and experiences, I thought:

I wish everyone felt this at home in our churches, so unquestionably a part of our communities, so joyous about all the things we do when we gather. Would that the entire world felt the embrace of the church like many a PK, like my children have through the years and in multiple congregations. When my children were this little girl's age, I served a small congregation in rural North Carolina and that church's covered dish lunches were legendary. And not only my kids, but all the kids of that small fellowship, were always at the front of the line, hovering with plates in hand as I prayed over the meal. The children ate first, returned to the dessert table often and wandered freely. And I imagine these feasts mirrored the heavenly banquet.

I like to think our gatherings are earthly versions of the promised heavenly ones, at least in part, anyway. They are, after all, a household of God family meals where all manner of people come to the table and the little children are at the front of the line. They are places where no one sits alone, and everyone gets their fill. There are always leftovers. People take turns setting up and making the iced tea. Another group washes dishes. Everyone brings whatever they have to share and if you happen to show up without something — no problem, there is more than enough, everyone is invited to eat. Little kids wander around, various adults tend to them, there is no head table and going back for seconds is encouraged.

This sounds heavenly to me, especially right now in this pandemic time when we cannot be together.

Don't you yearn for those slightly chaotic, random casserole, so-much-food, church suppers? Don't you miss being in the sanctuary, seated beside each other, passing the silver trays of tiny cubes of bread and juggling the bulky ones with the little cups of juice? Don't you wish we could be at the feast of our Lord and the banquet of God together today?

I feel something in this longing that I can only describe as homesickness. I miss looking out and seeing you in your respective pews and hugging you in the narthex and catching up over a plate of mac and cheese and that congealed salad that only appears in the fellowship hall. I want to follow my princess tour guide down the halls and around the corners and through the staircase and into the choir loft in all the church buildings that often make no architectural sense because they were built too many decades apart often with not quite enough money to do what was actually planned.

I want to sit at a table with you and be as comfortable in that space as every young PK I know is in the church where their parent is a pastor. I miss being in church, together, because the church gathered is so worth missing, because you, the church, have given me so much and loved not just me, but my children and not just my children but countless others' children and not just children but all manner of people, and not because we could really give you anything in return, but because you promised God you would.

That's what marks this covenant community we know as church at its best, often in fits and starts, never without the help of the Spirit; it is an outpost of grace and mercy and unconditional love. The church is a place where everyone is invited to come to the table, to be fed, to have their fill and go back for seconds, to eat even if they didn't bring anything to the gathering. In short: to be welcomed and honored because they are beloved of God. This, my friends, is remarkable, perhaps especially now.

Now, I know, yes, I know we get it wrong and we fail miserably at this call to welcome all. We too often are both in and of the world and too often reflect the values of our culture rather than offer a counter example. It takes very little research, just some brief reading of session minutes to reveal how often we have turned people away, exploited those Jesus told us to serve and injured the already vulnerable. We need to be honest about our failings, our sin, and the evil in which we've participated. We need to look clearly around our tables and note where we are sitting, who is serving, and who is absent. We need to repent and ask the Spirit to intervene and help us do better, because we not only insult God when we reject others, we diminish the beauty and joy of the Lord's Supper. We withhold the gift of grace that is not ours, that we hold in trust, that we are to steward by sharing, a gift that grows and gets better the more lavishly it is given. Everyone ought to know what it is like to be invited, welcomed and honored, everyone ought to know the truth that there is a place at God's table with their name on it and our feast won't be the same without them.

I miss communion in the sanctuary and meals in the fellowship hall. I miss being together with my church family. I imagine you wanted to welcome your new pastor in ways you couldn't. But what I want to say to you in that, there is a blessing embedded in this longing. And that blessing is this: You know the church, the Body of Christ, the household of God, the communion of the saints is well worth missing. You know that while Zoom is great and phone calls are wonderful and worshiping in our yoga pants has its perks, there is something, something ineffable and powerful, about being together that cannot be replicated or replaced. You know what it means to have a literal place at the Lord's table, at the church's table, at one another's table. You know what it means to have a meal made and brought to you, to serve and be served, to not only eat but be fed and nourished. You know what it is like to be unquestionably home in the house of God and there is nothing else like it.

But, friends, there are so many of God's beloved children who do not know what that is like. They do not know their way around the sanctuary or how to get to the fellowship hall. They do not know what it feels like to have someone tell them to go to the front of the line, to be our guest, to come as they are and be truly, completely, utterly welcomed. They don't feel like they are at home, that they have a home in the household of God, in the body of Christ, in the communion of the saints, in the church, or even in the world.

This season of so many challenges, so much acrimony, and such relentless hurting, reveals the need to expand our tables and show the limitless love of God. Just like those church suppers, we need to trust without a doubt that there is enough for everyone, that there will be baskets left over, that we have plenty to share; so much, in fact, that we need to go out and invite others to the banquet so that this glorious feast doesn't go to waste.

As I was leaving that church in Georgia, I followed the other PK, a few years younger than his sister, out of the building. But just before we exited, he stopped, turned to me and told me the security code for the door. "You know, so you can come back whenever you want to."

And I do want to go back. I long for the day when it is safe for us all to be back, together, around the communion table, and in the fellowship hall and on folding chairs in Sunday school rooms, and when that time comes, I pray I will bring others with me because they may not know what they are missing, but I sure do and I know you do, too. So now is the time to start making invitations, seeking out those who need to know they are valued and wanted. Right now, as you begin this new phase of your journey, in this season of our life together, our call is to let everyone know they have a place of honor at God's table and we have the joyous privilege of showing them to their seat — princess costume optional. Amen.

Proper 18 / Ordinary Time 23
Luke 14:25-33

Calculated Christianity

Grit is trending these days. Have you heard of it? There was a viral TED talk by Angela Duckworth in 2013 and then she published a book of the same title in 2018 — *Grit: The Power Of Passion And Perseverance.* In a nutshell, "grit" is mental toughness, the ability to persevere and keep at it in order to achieve a long-term goal. Like calculating what it is going to take to build that big tower and then keeping after it, no matter that a storm knocked it down or that the permit got delayed or that thieves stole the materials, just keep calculating and working until it stands tall for all to see and admire.

Is this calculated Christianity, this determined discipleship, about grit? Is Jesus telling us to be gritty followers?

There is a big part of me that wants this to be the case because, well, I am Presbyterian, and I am from Scot-Irish, born fighting, Presbyterians. We are known for our grit, right? My parents' mantra to me throughout my entire childhood was: BUCK UP. In my family, we take pride in the stories of our ancestors who jumped off a boat and swam to shore in order to escape authorities, the ones who crawled on their hands and knees picking berries to help feed their families, the ones who climbed up the economic ladder through mental toughness and hard work. We like to epitomize that Protestant work ethic.

When our oldest was in kindergarten and he had an assignment to create a family belief statement, we thought we'd be really creative and write an acrostic poem using the letters of our last name. (We were eager, he was the first.) So, we started with "D" and "thought 'How about 'determined'?" "D" is for determined. But wanting to include the student we asked our son, "Joseph, do

Proper 18 / Ordinary Time 23

you know what determined means?" And he said, "I think so. It's when you try and try until you know you can't do it." Clearly, we had work to do on nurturing his grit.

Is that what Jesus was doing there — encouraging godly grit?

Was Jesus admonishing the crowd to be determined disciples?

Was Jesus calling the crowds to mental toughness, knowing all Jerusalem loomed in the distance?

Was calculated Christianity all about our gut-it-out, stick-to-it, never-give-up, grit?

Or could it be Jesus wanted us to make intentional choices, to be informed, and smart.

Maybe this calculated Christianity is more like that popular coaching method that employs SMART goals. Have you heard of them?

It is an acronym for:

Specific, Measurable, Attainable, Relevant, and Timely.

Is calculated Christianity, small-print, full disclosure, all-in-faith about setting SMART goals and sticking with them?

Would it be something like — I will donate ten items of clothing in order to be closer to Jesus' admonishment to give up my possessions. I will measure this by counting out ten items of clothing and taking them to Goodwill. This is attainable because, let's face it, I have a lot of items of clothing in my closet, many of them don't even spark joy, and I need more room anyway. It is relevant because Jesus says we need to get rid of our stuff. I will do this by the end of September — boom — timely.

Is this what Jesus meant when he said to estimate the expenditure, and figure out what it would take? Did he mean to do a detailed faith pro forma? Did he mean to be able to measure, quantify, and count the cost of discipleship?

I hope so, because I can do this. The other parts about hating my parents, spouse, and kids, I don't find these attainable or frankly all that specific. I mean there are moments when I feel an acute irritation, but hate is a strong word and is this not counter to all love verses in scripture? Love God, love neighbor, they will know you are my followers by your love, faith, hope, and love abide, these three but the greatest of these is love, perfect love casts out fear, God is love. Jesus was sending a mixed message here.

Could we just go with some Christian SMART goals and still be counted among Jesus' followers? It would look great in our stewardship materials and our end of the year reports. We could even publicize them and put some of those big graphs, a thermometer perhaps in the narthex that shows where we are in meeting them. We could watch it inch up, week to week, and feel good about our progress, know exactly where we stand.

Increase giving this fiscal year by 5%. Specific, measurable, perhaps attainable, relevant, of course, timely, yes.

How's that, Jesus? Intentional, informed, no one will ridicule us, they may well look to us as one of those "best practices" places; discipleship: sorted.

We can be gritty, determined, and SMART and therefore surely counted among Jesus' followers, right? But what do we do about that troublesome language about hating those closest to us, the very ones we'd lay down our life for? What about that odd call to hate our life that sounds downright pathological in a culture awash in talk and titles of self-love, life balance, and self-care? Does God really require us to hate that which we most cherish?

When Jesus turned to those crowds drawn to his healings and authoritative teachings, his compassion, and his miracles, and told them: "Whoever comes to me and does not hate father and mother, wife and children, brothers and sisters, yes, and even life itself, cannot be my disciple. Whoever does not carry the cross and follow me cannot be my disciple" he was asking them, and us, to do the impossible and perhaps that is exactly the point.

It is exactly the point because calculated Christianity is not about our grit or our smarts. It is about surrendering to God's will, power, grace, compassion, mercy, and love.

Discipleship is not about what we can attain, it is about what God in Christ does for us and through us and sometimes despite us. It is about knowing that we will try and try and try until we know we can't do it, not on our own. We will try to be faithful, try to be forgiving, try to live a life worthy of the calling to which we have been called, try to do what we know is right but inevitably get to a place where we do the very thing we hate anyway and then we know we cannot do it. There is not enough grit and good works in the world to make us worthy to be counted among Jesus' followers, but yet, we are. We will never be smart enough to know the mind of God because our thoughts are not God's thoughts. And yet we are promised that Christ makes his home in our hearts.

We are the clay and God is the potter. Faithful discipleship is about being shaped by the most high God again and again. It is not about our righteousness or abilities, our successes or our failures, it is about trusting and seeking to follow the one who came to save sinners. Discipleship is not about avoiding the ridicule of others, but being a fool for Christ. Discipleship is not demonstrating our might and subduing our enemies, it is about sacrificial service that turns the other cheek. How do we measure the price and the impact of these things? Which one of you, of us, could possibly do them without the help of the One through whom all things are possible?

Jesus' admonishment to the crowds and to us is a call to calculate the cost so that we know only he can pay the price. Only then will we live our lives in joyous gratitude for Jesus' sacrifice, for the amazing grace that meets us where we are but never leaves us as we've been found.

I cannot hate my parents or my spouse or my kids and my life is far too filled with blessings for me to be anything but grateful. But I know I can only love them all rightly when I put Jesus Christ first, when I recognize and know to the marrow of my bones that I have been saved by grace, when I want nothing more and nothing less than to surrender to God's good will even though I know I will try and try and try and fail, but God will forgive and forgive and forgive and use me anyway.

The possessions I most need to surrender are not only material but the false gods; false stories, false pride, and pretenses to which

The Upside Down, Backwards Life of Disciples

I cling most closely: like grit and self-righteousness, the illusion that I am smart, that my privileges are somehow earned, that I am entitled to what I have, that I can somehow accurately calculate and measure and evaluate my Christianity, my faithfulness, my discipleship or anyone else's. When I let go of these things, I yield to be shaped in ways pleasing to God and useful to others.

The truth is, I could give away all I own and still not make a dent in the debt I owe the One who went to the cross in my stead.

We can never calculate what discipleship requires, we can only surrender to the potter and be shaped in surprising ways that God will use beyond all we could ever imagine or do on our own, no matter how determined we are.

Which one of you could ever calculate the value of knowing Jesus Christ? Discipleship, both the gift and the responsibility of it, is priceless, all we can do is offer God whatever we have, in faith and humility, trusting that Jesus will take it, bless it, and shape it for the building of his kingdom and his victory over everything that could separate us from his love. That's the formula for following Jesus and, thanks be to God, the only calculation that truly matters. Amen.

Proper 19 / Ordinary Time 24
Luke 15:1-10

Where's The One?

Over the past few weeks, I've heard some variation of the following over and over again: "I'm craving some good news." "I am longing for beauty." "I'm tired of feeling beaten up and not good enough." Maybe you've heard versions of these sentiments, too. Or maybe you have expressed them. I'm not sure why I'm hearing this from so many sources now, but I can guess it is because there is so much bad news, so much ugliness, so many people willing to be critical, pointing out flaws in themselves, their friends and the famous alike. There seems no escape from news reports of men, women and children writhing in pain after a chemical weapons attach perpetrated by their own government. There are headlines in the city where my mother lives of a woman in her early sixties, a teacher, murdered by her husband after twice being refused a restraining order against him. The local news is filled with conflict over homelessness: how to deal with the issue, how to help people, how to be faithful to those trying to go about life and work, knowing that if the answer were easy we wouldn't find ourselves in the place we are in virtually every city in America.

Bad news, ugliness, feeling overwhelmed and beaten up, not good enough, not compassionate enough, not adequate enough, such sentiments seem to be in the air and water these days. For me, it was a dog that almost pushed me over the existential edge. It was a stray dog that threatened to paralyze my hope and make me want to throw up my hands and give up on striving to make the world a better place.

I was in Nashville earlier this week and I got up early to go for a walk. It was my only opportunity to get a glimpse of the city where I was doing some work. I was enjoying being in the shadow of Vanderbilt, blissfully unaware of the looming football game, by the way, when I saw a dog, skinny, dirty, and sniffing around a trash can. It looked like some sort of golden retriever mix and as I got closer, I saw it had a chain collar on, but as far as I could tell, no tag. I guess he was lost or abandoned; clearly, he'd had a home at some point. I tried to get closer to him, called to him, cajoled him, but he was afraid and the closer I got the faster he went in the opposite direction. I kept walking and saw him later hanging around the divinity school dorm, when a young, tender-hearted seminary student came out waving a slice of last night's pizza just close enough to get the untrusting pup's attention.

Even so, I could not get that darn dog out of my head. He made me sad in that global sense of nothing is right with the world, sad. The dog, the lost or abandoned dog! Not the war in Syria, not homelessness, not the fact that we have no cure for Alzheimer's or cancer, not people who've lost their communities due to fire, famine of floods, but one pitiful dog gave me a sense of desperation. That darn dog made me crave good news, made me long for beauty, made me feel wholly beaten up and helpless.

There is something about the *one*: one creature, one person, one story that points us to the whole. And, for whatever reason, this one dog pointed me to the whole of lostness and hurt. But as I thought about it, I wondered if there was something important in the sadness that one dog evoked. I wondered if maybe, just maybe, buried in the 'kicked in the gut' feeling for the one, there is the promise of hope and rejoicing for the all.

I wonder if that is what is going on in these stories. Jesus went after the *one*. He leaves the 99, and surely those 99 had needs, too. But he left the 99 to go after the *one* that was desperate to be restored to community, to wholeness, and to a safe place where care can be given. Maybe Jesus, even though he was responding to those sneering, grumbling Pharisees and scribes, maybe he was telling his disciples, "Look for the one and bring it back to the ninety-nine." Perhaps Jesus was acknowledging that we are

Proper 19 / Ordinary Time 24

easily overwhelmed by the cries of the whole flock, that we are quick to throw up our hands and say, "What difference can we make?" in the face of so much hurt, ugly, and suffering. So he said, "Well, I've got the whole world in my hands. I am the Good Shepherd. I know the hairs on the heads of them all, so you ask yourselves, where is the one?" Perhaps that's why that one breaks our hearts. That story of the one child in poverty, the one elderly woman choosing between buying her medicine or her groceries, the one man who lost the job he held for thirty years, the one friend going through a divorce, and the one co-worker struggling with a chronic illness. Jesus said, "Where is that *one*?" Think for a minute. Who is the one you know, right now, who needs to be sought out and brought back and cared for?

It might be someone on the pew with you. It may be someone in your own household or family. Some days it may well be you. It could be one issue you are passionate about or one place in the world you feel compelled to help. Jesus says to you and to me, "Where's the one?" Do you have it? It's okay if it is you or your next door neighbor or the person you've not seen in church for a while. The Spirit works in all of this, intercedes, advocates, counsels. Jesus asks you, "Where is the one?" Don't overthink what or who comes to your consciousness. Do you have the one?

Now do one thing, one thing to seek out that one. Think of one thing that one may need to hear or know or feel. It does not have to be grand, and it is okay if that one is you today. That one thing for that one who God has placed before you may be to pray for that person or situation. You may be called to lift them up to God in prayer. Do not discount that. It may be that you are called to pick up the phone or write them a note or send them a text message. Do they need a meal? Or help with childcare? Do they need a job? Or an invitation to come to your Sunday school class? It may not seem grand, but here's the amazing thing about God's kingdom economy — nothing is wasted. God takes whatever we offer in faith, blesses and uses it, often in ways we will never see or know. Hasn't that been true in your own life? Aren't there people who have said something to you or done something for

The Upside Down, Backwards Life of Disciples

you when you needed it most that have no idea the impact it made?

Jesus said, "Where's the one?" and then he asked, "What's the one thing that will help bring them home?" Here's the exceedingly good news, the beauty of seeking out and finding the one: We get to rejoice together when that one is brought back into the fold. We get to celebrate, throw a party, with all the other 99. It means that we should be rejoicing every single day, at every homecoming of every one who returns to the flock. It means we are privy to and a part of seemingly small victories that, in reality, are huge.

I know a woman who volunteers with an organization that uses horses, caring for them, riding them, to help reach children with a wide range of challenges. Some of the children have autism. Others are physically disabled. Some have behavior problems at school. This particular woman's one passion is this work. She volunteers one day a week. She works with one child at a time. The children often participate for months and some for years. She told me about one little boy she's worked with since he was in pre-school. He has autism. He does not speak. At first, he would run from the horses. He would run into the arena and write large letters in the dust. The volunteer would follow him when he ran. She would let him write in the dirt. She would walk him back and try again to get him to ride the horse. She purchased a box of large cardboard letter so he could spell out things like "mounting block" and "horse." This went on for months, running, finding, and bringing back. Then, one day, driving to the stables from the backseat of the car this non-verbal child said to his mother, "I ride pony." And he did. And he does. Three words, that's it, from one boy, but you can imagine the rejoicing with everyone in that family and everyone at that stable, when that one was brought back and didn't run away again.

That's the good news, the profound beauty, the *enoughness* with God's help, of seeking out the one and bringing that one back: We get to rejoice, over and over and over again, together and with the whole company of heaven, angels, and God and the risen Christ included. So, ask yourself, where is the one? And go find them so we can rejoice together. Amen.

Proper 20 / Ordinary Time 25
Luke 16:1-13

Give Me Your Word

I am telling the truth. I am not lying. Believe me. It seems every newscast contains a story about truth telling these days. We are in the throes of the election season and talk of "fact checking" abounds. Politifact has the "Truth-O-Meter" (a term that they have trademarked, by the way) that ranks candidates' statements anywhere from true to half-truth to pants on fire. There is talk of "transparency" ad nauseam, not only in the government but in the church. The Presbyterian Mission Agency Board just wrapped up their meeting in Louisville and part of their time together was devoted to a "generative discussion" on the "purpose of transparency." I am telling the truth, I am not lying.

Discussions about telling the truth and transparency bubble up when trust has been breached, or has been perceived to be, anyway. And so it is in this odd, odd story from Luke this morning. This is a story about truth telling, about transparency. The man is called to the office where his master says, "What is this I have heard about you… you can no longer be my manager." Things are not looking good. It is that "oh, gosh" moment. The email that you inadvertently "replied all" has been read. Your phone was not on mute during the conference call. There was a surveillance camera and look, there you are, when you said you weren't. Your alibi busted. The Facebook post was not as private as those private settings led you to believe. Delete doesn't mean what you thought it meant.

What is this I hear about you? Give me the account.

The master, the boss, the parent, or principal, the person with a great deal of power over your fate and your future says, "Give me your word."

The Upside Down, Backwards Life of Disciples

Now it is our turn to talk. What will we say? We could lie and let the fact checkers and truth-o-meters do their work, let the chips fall where they may. Maybe they don't know what I think they know. I've done that, we've seen others do that. Maybe the evidence isn't as irrefutable as it appears. Let's roll the dice and see what happens!

But this scripture passage is instructive. It speaks of the dishonest manager, the shrewd or prudent manager, if you like. He didn't do that. When the master said: "Give me your word," the manager had a revelation, a moment of honest self-awareness, that didn't allow him to say, "I didn't do it, I swear. I am not lying, believe me."

He assessed his situation and determined it was pretty dire. I am not strong enough to dig. I am too proud to beg. I don't have a plan B or a golden parachute. I can't afford a really good attorney. What now?

It is fascinating in Luke ho w many people talk to themselves and what they say and what happens as a result of their ability to be honest. Just a few verses back the prodigal "comes to himself" and realized he'd rather be a servant in his father's house than live like he was living. He wasn't too proud to beg and he was willing to be a servant instead of a son.

A few chapters before that we have the guy with his big barns, remember him? He talked to himself, too. But he said something different. He saw all his possessions and thought all he needed to do was build a secure place for them and then, he told himself, he would eat, drink, and be merry. He didn't need to dig, he had no reason to beg, but he wound up dead anyway.

In a few chapters hence we get Zacchaeus, that wee little man, and in his come-to-Jesus moment he says, "If I have cheated anyone I am going to give it back four-fold and while I am at it I am going to give half my possessions to the poor."

The rich young ruler — when he is face to face with the one who holds his fate and his future — he is honest, too. "Sorry, Jesus, I just can't do it. If it is my money or my life, I pick my money."

Proper 20 / Ordinary Time 25

The word we give when we are called to give an account of ourselves has consequences. When the master says "Give me your word," what do we say?

When Jesus said, "What is this I hear about you?" and we know it hasn't all been good, because it is never all good, how will we respond? How honest will we be, with ourselves, with others, and with God?

Give me your word. Is what I hear about you true?

Yes, Lord — every last syllable!

I am not strong enough to dig.

I am too proud to beg.

I have squandered what you entrusted to me.

I have taken my inheritance and blown it on instant gratification and exploited others in the process.

I looked out for number one and then justified it every day and twice on Sundays.

You desired mercy, I demanded sacrifices.

I rejoiced at the suffering of others and resented the success of people I should have celebrated.

I have not loved or prayed for my enemies. I rarely turned the other cheek.

I hurt the people closest to me the most. Sometimes I hurt them knowingly.

I knew better, but did what I hated anyway.

I built bigger barns, I failed to see Lazarus at the gate, or if I did, I ignored him.

I deserted you in the garden and denied you by the fire, not once but three times.

I have sinned against heaven and against you. I am not worthy to be your child.

I give you my word — painful as it is. But I am not strong enough to dig, I am too proud to beg. All I can do is go out and do more of what I did that got me in this predicament in the first place.

That's the kicker, right? This guy got caught red-handed and what did he do? He went out and cheated some more. Sound

The Upside Down, Backwards Life of Disciples

familiar? Have you ever sworn up and down that you've learned your lesson, that you are truly sorry and you humbly repent, then darned if you don't go out in all that sincerity and sin some more? But listen to this story from Luke. Notice what happened. When he got called back to the office, he got commended, not condemned! Grace abounds. Even with all the messiness of our questionable motives and impure actions — grace abounds.

That's the point. The ones who work the least get paid as much as the ones who worked the longest. The prodigal got celebrated, not castigated. Jesus called tax collectors and sinners. The dishonest manager was called prudent. None of us get what we deserve. It's called grace, but too often we resent it rather than replicate it.

When we give our word, when we are called to account, when we say, *Lord God, this is our story and unfortunately, we have no choice but to stick to it. I am no longer worthy to be called your son. I have sinned against heaven and against you. I have been a lousy steward and not the best of neighbors either,* Jesus says, "Well, guess what? I came to save sinners and you qualify."

We never get what we deserve. We get grace. We get forgiveness. We are given purpose. We are offered reconciliation and not a second chance but a third and a fourth and seventy-times-seven. God's Word, the Word made flesh, the One who dwells among us, the Word of life, speaks for us, intercedes for us, prays for us, changes the ending to our account, commends rather than condemns, welcomes instead of rejects, makes our denials the very foundations of others affirmations of faith.

When we are called to account, face-to-face with the one who holds our fate and our future and asked to give our word, our utterly, soul-bearing, honest word, God responds with the Word and we don't get what we deserve. We get grace.

And maybe part of the point of this strange story is the dishonest manager's prudence. On behalf of the master, he extends grace to others. What do you owe? Cut it in half. What about you? Let's call it even. You know what, today, I am going to give you a break. No seriously. Just pay what you can. Maybe

Proper 20 / Ordinary Time 25

that's a lesson to take from today, too. God desires everyone be saved. There is one God, one mediator, Jesus Christ. Grace abounds. Grace should beget grace — even with all of our mixed motives, questionable intentions and imperfect actions. Could that be our response to the mercy shown to us? Could we practice not calculating what others deserve and instead intentionally, systematically, relentlessly practice grace? Forgive our debtors as our debts have been forgiven?

In this age of internet justice, when shaming is a national pastime and demonizing as easy as a share or a post, this would be a radical departure for us. But man, would it be freeing. What if we took a page out of the Jesus' play book and stopped hoping people would get what they deserve and instead desired mercy for everyone and extended grace to all.

A few weeks ago I heard a story on the radio about a woman whose prison sentence was commuted.[1]

The announcer said:

> *And let's hear now from one woman who had her sentence commuted just over a year ago. Her name is Shauna Barry-Scott, and she spent ten years in prison...*
>
> *She was sentenced to twenty years for possession with intent to distribute cocaine. Prison, she says, was a nightmare. She saw overcrowding, medical neglect, abuse from guards. One day, she got called to the warden's office.*
>
> BARRY-SCOTT: *So I said, oh, god, I'm really in big trouble now. They're sending me to the warden. So I'm sitting there and after quite a while, my unit manager walked in and my counselor. And me and my counselor were real close. He wasn't mean like some of the other people there were. And when he walked through that door, he had this big, giant smile on his face. And when I saw his smile, it just hit me. I said, oh, my god, this must*

---

[1] https://www.npr.org/2016/08/31/492057138/prisoners-granted-clemency-must-adjust-to-new-lives

The Upside Down, Backwards Life of Disciples

be the clemency. And sure enough, the warden started to tell me that I had received it...

She continued: *When you go to prison, you are stripped of every bit of your dignity, your place in society. And you lose, I think, some of your humanity with it. So after being gone for so long, I kind of didn't know, you know, where I fit into the scheme of things anymore.*

But she is figuring it out and finding solace in the small things.

BARRY-SCOTT: *The other morning, I had a moment (laughter). My kids were all gone. And I made some toast and poured some coffee in a cup. And it just dawned on me that just even to be able to use a toaster in my own kitchen — I was just a little overwhelmed.*

Our sentence has been commuted. We've been granted clemency. Our humanity has been restored. We've been set free. It is a little overwhelming. What are we going to do? Who will we serve? How will we live? Well, we could start with the small things, give thanks for those, be faithful in those and trust God's Word of grace confident that we never get what we deserve. Grace abounds, not just for us, for everyone. I am telling the truth, I am not lying. Amen.

Proper 21 / Ordinary Time 26
Luke 16:19-31

The Great Divide

Recently, I attended two birthday parties just several days apart. One was simple. There was a cake, two small gifts: a frisbee and a set of sheets, to be exact. It was a party for a boy turning ten. The boy was serenaded by his family and a group of relative strangers, some of whom, including me, had just learned his name. The party took place in the fellowship hall of a church, the boy's home on this particular week. The next party was perhaps a little over the top. There were eleven small children gathered at the Build-A-Bear® workshop in the mall. Each child made a bear, dressed it, and took it home in a box that contained candy and stickers. Each child had supper and cake in the mall food court. They got a prize in their kid's meal and a bright balloon. There were lots of gifts for the birthday girl, some of which have yet to be played with because the little girl has many things. She needs no sheets for her bed. She has plenty. Her home is safe and spacious. She doesn't share a bedroom. Her toys, and those of her siblings, take up space in virtually every room in the house. There have been times when her mother has gathered up numerous large bags of toys and taken them to Goodwill and these children have not even known they were gone. I know because I am that mother and the birthday party was for my daughter who just turned four.

The first party I described took place the week our church hosted the Interfaith Hospitality Network. For those who are unfamiliar with this program, it is a national organization with local affiliates. It helps homeless families work toward permanent housing and churches volunteer to host the families once a quarter for one week. The churches provide dinner and space for the families to sleep. It is a wonderful program with a successful track record. My family provided dinner one night. We came and ate together and played with the children and visited with their parents. We celebrated a young boy's birthday. And as we did, I couldn't help but compare his celebration with the one I knew was coming up for my daughter. The comparison was striking. One was sumptuous, the other very simple. And I wonder if both, or either, were pleasing to God.

Could it please God to know that even one of his children is homeless in a land where the vast majority dress in purple and fine linen? Could it please God to know that there is such a great divide between what my children have and what the children sleeping in our churches have? Could it possibly please God to see that stuffed bears are dressed better than many children around the world? Likely, it would not. Such great divisions are never pleasing to God. God knows and loves all children and to see some suffer while others feast does not sit well with such a God.

And yet, those divisions are not the entire story of either party. God does love both those at the feast and those at the gate. And I have to ask: Does it please God to see friends and family and yes, even strangers gather together to celebrate the life and birth of one of his own? Does it please God to see churches open their doors and use their resources to reach out to others? Does it please God to hear a child delight in opening a present given from the heart? Does it please God for children to play, laugh, and enjoy themselves? Does it please God for parents to want to show their child they relish the day they were born? Of course it does. God knows and loves all children and to see them valued and cherished, whether in church halls or shopping malls must bring God pleasure.

The problem lies not in the sumptuousness of my daughter's party, but in the fact that such a party is so inaccessible to so many. The problem is that many kids don't even get a cake in a borrowed church hall and too often we don't even seem to notice. Or if we notice we don't seem to care. Lazarus longs to satisfy his hunger from the crumbs that fall from the rich man's table. The crumbs, just the crumbs, would have been enough to sustain and satisfy him, yet the rich man doesn't even see fit to give him those. The divide is great and the chasm between them is being fixed. So too it is with us and many of our brothers and sisters. This year in the United States, close to 20% of all children under age five are living in poverty. That means a family of four living on less than $18,200 a year and 5.1 million children in the United States live in "extreme" poverty. That is defined as a household income of less than half that amount. The US Department of Agriculture says that 10.7% of US households cannot always afford the food they need. This is in the United States. The numbers are vastly more in the vast majority of the rest of the world. Friends, the crumbs from our tables could make a big difference in bridging this great divide.

God cares. This text clearly tells us God cares. God cares about Lazarus, God cares about the rich man, God cares about my daughter and the boy sleeping in the church Sunday school room. God cares about me and about you. God cares how we treat one another. What we do here and now matters immeasurably to God. And ultimately, I can't enjoy the sumptuous feast, the real sumptuous feast, the feast that God sacrificed his son for and to which all are invited to come and be filled, unless I open up my table and share here and now.

We have to begin to bridge the great divide between people or the chasm between us and God will be fixed and no amount of pleading will reunite us. So, where do we start? First, we recognize that Lazarus is at our gate. We see him, we speak to him, and we acknowledge that he too is a beloved child of God, worthy of our attention and care. Next, perhaps we read carefully the instructions in 1 Timothy and get our priorities straight. We find ways to pursue righteousness, godliness, faith, love, endurance, and gentleness. We learn to not compare ourselves to others but to be content with food and clothing. We try to be rich in good works, generous, and ready to share. We remind ourselves daily that we brought nothing into the world and we'll take nothing out of it and that everything we have ultimately belongs to God. We ask ourselves often, is this a faithful use of God's provisions to me? Will this increase the great divide or build a bridge between it?

God does not begrudge my daughter her teddy bear, but God does grieve that other children don't have one. God calls us to grieve together and then invite those children to the party, too. We see Lazarus and the gate and we find him offensive and scary. We want to turn away, ignore him, and lock the gate. But God says, *no, you have to speak, call him by name in this life and share what's on your table*. There will be enough. There is always enough when we recognize that God is really the host and we're all just guests thanks to God's grace.

Our family provided dinner and played with the children and visited with the parents at the Interfaith Hospitality Network on a Thursday night. My son, on our way out of the church, said, "That was fun, can we come back again tomorrow?" And we did. And we played, we visited, and we celebrated a little boy's birthday. The children of the network and the children of the church played cards, tag, and football. They got cake on their hands, icing on their lips, and they laughed. They called each other by name and were worn completely out when it was time for bed. Some headed to bunk beds with matching sheets and comforters in color coordinated rooms and some to air mattresses in Sunday school classrooms with tables pushed aside. All were and are beloved by God. The divide didn't feel so great, the chasm not yet fixed. My daughter hugged the birthday boy's sister and asked if they could play together again. "Sure," I said. "Well, get her phone number," my daughter said impatiently. And I was reminded that the gate was still there and that it was my job to work to keep it from closing so that we can all play together again. I know that would be pleasing to God. Amen.

Proper 22 / Ordinary Time 27
Luke 17:5-10

Upside Down And Backward

We get it backward, this life of faith, this discipleship, this Jesus following. We look at things from a perspective of what we lack, rather than through the lens of abundance. God gives us more than enough to do the work we are called to do. We are promised that God will do abundantly more than we hope or imagine. Jesus gifts us with the Holy Spirit to give us the right words at the right time. That Spirit intercedes for us, Christ prays for us and still we stand paralyzed, begging Jesus to increase our faith.

We get it backward, seeing scarcity when God follows us and chases us down with goodness and mercy all the days of our lives.

We get it upside down, too by making ourselves those to be served, rather than the servants. We seek worldly status and earthly power when Jesus says plainly, repeatedly, the last will be first and the first will be last. Jesus told us if we are to enter the kingdom we must become like children. Jesus said he is not only with the least of these, but, in fact, is the least of these, the hungry and imprisoned, the naked and shunned.

The Jesus way is an odd way, a strange way not conformed to this world but transformed through the love of our God who claims and calls us, names and sends us. It tells us to go to the ends of the earth baptizing and teaching, preaching and healing, carrying nothing with us but instead relying on the hospitality of strangers. His way asks of us not that which we do not have, but only to willingly gift to God whatever we possess, trusting that God will take it, bless it, use it to show others their true worth, their holy goodness, their divine-image-dignity.

The Upside Down, Backwards Life of Disciples

The life of faith is a backward, upside down existence that calls attention to itself by its strangeness. Those who claim to follow Jesus are known by our love, not our power, our giving, not our hoarding, our grace, not our grudge-holding. When we really emulate our Savior we stand out, look naïve, even foolish to a cynical world enamored with vengeance and suspicious of mercy.

No wonder we ask Jesus to increase our faith in the face of such an upside down and backward vocation, a life that looks radically different than the worldly values in which it is so often lived. To say you want to be great resonates in our culture. We brag about the power of pride and the glory of being self-made people. We celebrate the rich and envy the powerful. We base our value and that of others on net worth or lack thereof and do little to level the playing field in what we pretend is a pure meritocracy. We do not only ask Jesus to increase our faith, we pray to God to increase our bank account. Bigger is better, a sure sign of a blessing from God, we assume. We do not relish being relegated to positions of service but rather strive to be those waited on and given special consideration when we walk in the door.

But Jesus turned all of this upside down and backward. Jesus came and upended the money changers' tables. He came to set the captives free. His mother Mary sang of the proud being brought down and the lowly lifted up. Jesus not only ate with sinners and tax collectors, he called them to participate in God's present and coming kingdom. He welcomed little children, touched the untouchable, went to the graveyard to tell the demon possessed he had a name and a purpose.

No wonder the apostles asked Jesus to increase their faith. Those first followers weren't the elites of their day. They had no sway in the halls of power, no reason to believe anyone would listen to them, every reason to think they would be ignored, silenced or persecuted. Can we blame them for wanting some extra reassurance and an additional measure of holy hope?

The upside down and backward life is not for the faint of heart. Not then, not now. Faith is the assurance of things hoped for, the certainty of things not seen, right? Who would not need more of that kind of confidence?

But here is the great mystery of this peculiar Christian calling. It is in dying to self that we become fully alive. It is in pouring ourselves out that we are filled with the Holy Spirit. It is in serving that we discover true greatness. It is in following Jesus that we become God's leaders in the world. It is in acting out of our mustard seed sized faith that God moves mountains through us.

The only way to discover these bizarre truths, however, is to begin to live them. Our temptation to desire more before we step out in faith is perpetual. We want to build bigger barns, have just a little more savings and security and then we will be generous. We promise, Lord. We want just a little more influence and power, a small buffer from what may be egregious consequences, before we speak truth to power. Just let my children get a bit older — my career a bit father along. I need just one more class or perhaps another degree and then I will be qualified to do what God wants me to do. After all, I am just a tax collector, a fisherman, a mom, a janitor, or a business person or… . Lord, increase our faith and then… we really want to do your will, follow you closely, do justice, love kindness and walk humbly with you, but first, we need more… or we need different or, or, or.

But Jesus said incredulously, you have all you need and then some; with me you are far more than enough. You are not "just" anything, you are a beloved child of God, claimed, called, and sent. If you took that nascent faith, that tiniest molecule of faith, you could uproot the largest of shrubs and cast it into the sea. You could alter creation and turn evil upside down and make anything counter to the commandment to love God and neighbor seem utterly backward and wrong. Take that tiny bit of faith, offer it to God, use it in service to Jesus and trust that coupled with the power of God it will turn the world in ways that reflect the goodness and mercy of the One who created it.

In a world that always wants more, that acquires and consumes and then repeats this cycle endlessly, Jesus said, *enough*. You have

The Upside Down, Backwards Life of Disciples

enough. You have more than enough. Through Christ, all things are possible.

In a culture that all too often exploits those who serve, who refuses to pay a living wage to workers we have come to know as essential, Jesus said, *I am with them, I am them*. The Savior of the world came not to be served but to serve, how much more should his followers be eager to do likewise?

We need no increase of faith, we need only to act on the mustard seed amount God has placed within us. We do not need to be served and waited upon. We are called to show others what it means to be loved in tangible ways, through exercising radical hospitality in the name of Jesus Christ.

This discipleship life is upside down and backward, foolishness to the wise of this world, but to those of us called to follow Jesus Christ, it is glorious, salvific, and good. Utterly odd, absolutely beautiful, abundantly more than we could have ever hoped or imagined, possible through even mustard seed sized faith. Amen.

Proper 23 / Ordinary Time 28
Luke 17:11-19

The Power Of Proximity

Imagine being ostracized and isolated, forced to cry, "Unclean! Unclean!" wherever you went, commanded to make visible through your clothing and hair your already physically evident and painful condition. The writer of Luke said they should keep their distance. Those ten with leprosy didn't dare get close to Jesus, they called out for mercy from a distance. And Jesus, traveling to Jerusalem, between Samaria, that place with those people who refused to welcome him and Galilee, the region where so much of his ministry takes place, heard them, even from a distance. Even in this liminal space, with those still far off, headed to fulfill his divinely ordained purpose, Jesus heard those on the fringes of this world. He heard them and he responded with compassion.

Jesus would not let his ultimate, utterly critical, earth shattering, world saving, purpose thwart his tending to those in proximity to him all along the way. He was forever being interrupted. A random woman lunged at the hem of his garment and this while he was on the way to save a little girl. His interruptions got interrupted. He tried to go off to pray and disciples and needy people tracked him down. He attempted to teach and even though there wasn't an inch of space all around him some persistent people dug a hole in the roof to let down their ailing friend. Time and time again, no matter what he was doing, Jesus stopped and tended those the world ignores, overlooks and writes off.

Jesus heard, saw, and cared for those on the margins of our world, the outsider, outsiders, like lepers from Samaria. He unquestionably showed those long ostracized, isolated, demonized, and discarded that they were regarded, beloved, and worthy of not only the world's attention, but God's. If this is

The Upside Down, Backwards Life of Disciples

how Jesus, on the way to Jerusalem, responded, how much more ought we hear and respond to those calling out for mercy from a distance right now?

Those ten in that liminal space, geographically and socially, were relegated to an existence of mere survival, not abundant life. Jesus wouldn't stand for it, and neither should we.

Coming in proximity to the divine in our midst should transform cultural norms, upend revered religious rules and reverse what we thought were inevitable trajectories for ourselves and others. So powerful is this proximity to the Son of God that Jesus need only send these ten to the priest to show off their yet-to-be-cleansing and they are healed. All ten deserve credit for having even a modicum of faith, hope, and trust given their long suffering and perpetual exile. Despite their status and experience, they took Jesus at his word and did what he said. Even from a distance.

How often do we do likewise?

How often do I simply take Jesus at his word and do what he says?

How often do I risk anything, let alone everything, for the sake of the gospel? When have I sold my possessions, given the money to the poor and followed Jesus? How am I, really, welcoming the children? Am I visiting those in prison? Do I pray for my enemies? Seek the welfare of all those in the city where I live? Do I tend and feed Christ's sheep? Do I imagine that if I had faith the size of a mustard seed, I could move mountains? Do I really think that through Christ all things are possible? Do I believe through Christ something is possible?

Those ten, even from a distance, understood something about Jesus that I, a self-proclaimed follower, often fail to see. They understood the life-altering power of responding to his word, unequivocally, and with faith. If they, who were far off, took him at his word, how much more ought we, who are in this space, in such proximity as to be part of his body, the church, do likewise?

Imagine for a moment if we responded like those ten, even occasionally? What if, at our Bible studies, we ended each time

Proper 23 / Ordinary Time 28

with a commitment to try and do what Jesus says? I've shared with some of you a quote from Will Willimon that I try to keep in the forefront of my mind when I read scripture. It is this: "How would God have me to change in order to make this text believable?"[2]

Jesus said the last will be first and the first will be last. How would God have me to change in order to make this text believable? Jesus said, I desire mercy and not sacrifice. How would God have me to change in order to make this text believable? Jesus said, "I have come that you might have life and life abundant." How would God have me to change in order to make this text believable? Jesus said, "forgive seven times seventy times." How would God have me to change to make this text believable? "Blessed are the poor, the hungry, those who mourn," Jesus said. How would God have us to change in order to make this text believable? How do we respond to Jesus' word like the ten of this text?

Somehow, some way, those ten on the edges of society, with no reason in the world to trust the power and willingness of Jesus to heal, believed. They took him at his word and they went. Even the Samaritan, who had no obligation at all to go to the Jewish priest, did exactly as Jesus commanded.

If I ask myself: How would God have me to change in order to make this text believable? I need to remember that Jesus, when I was at a distance, came near to me, heard me, saw me, healed and saved me, through no merit of my own.

I need to stop, turn back, get close to Jesus, and worship him in order to really be well, not just aware of being cleansed, but astounded at being saved. I need the power of being in proximity to Jesus Christ, not occasionally, but daily.

I need to be close to Jesus Christ in order to be near to those he seeks out. I need to be in such proximity to the power of God that I witness the transformation it brings to people, and communities and again and again to me. I cannot just go to the temple, do the required religious rituals, and get on with my life. I need to

---

2 Will Willimon, *Proclamation and Theology* (Nashville, TN: Abingdon Press, 2005), 45.

The Upside Down, Backwards Life of Disciples

follow Jesus, daily, closely, in order to experience abundant life. That outsider, the Samaritan leper understood this, and when I remember, I do, too. When I remember what it was like to be an isolated fourth grader in a new country, afraid to open my mouth for fear the other kids would make fun of my Canadian accent, but the church ladies that welcomed me unconditionally each Sunday, I am moved to turn back to Jesus again. When I remember those times when grief threatened to consume me and somehow the peace of Christ found me, I want to go sit again at his feet. When I remember those seasons when I felt nothing more than the sum of my mistakes, but Jesus forgave me, I want to fall to the ground and give him praise. When I remember the occasions when I didn't feel enough or felt sure I didn't deserve a place at the table or wondered if the hurt I'd inflicted on those I care about the most could ever be used for good, and the love of God found a way, made plans for a future and gave me hope, I can't help but run back to the one who showed mercy when I had fallen so far from grace. The mercy of the Lord compels proximity to the one who gives it, when I remember, when I recognize the source of my salvation, stop and give God thanks.

Bryan Stevenson, founder of the Equal Justice Initiative, writes and speaks about the power of proximity to change our perspective, alter long entrenched narratives and enable us to really work for positive change. We can't participate in transformation from a distance. Following Jesus gets us close to people, especially those pushed furthest away from the centers of power and privilege. This proximity is inconvenient and uncomfortable, Stevenson said. But for those of us who've been found by the constantly interrupted, always upsetting those in power, crucified Savior, this ought not be a surprise. In fact, if we are too comfortable, we can be pretty sure we are one of the nine who were blessed but never turned back.

Stevenson, in his book *Just Mercy*, wrote, "The power of just mercy is that it belongs to the undeserving. It's when mercy is least expected that it's most potent — strong enough to break the cycle of victimization and victimhood, retribution and suffering."[3]

It is potent enough to bring us to the feet of the one who saves us, drawing us close with him to all those crying out at a distance for mercy, breaking the cycle of fear, estrangement, and bringing forth a revolution of reconciliation. That's the power of proximity to God and our neighbors that comes when we remember and recognize what Jesus has done for us and cannot help but turn back and follow him.

When I remember all that Jesus has done for me, when I see that even I've been cleansed and restored, redeemed and loved, I want to turn back, and get close enough to Jesus Christ, to be united with every tribe and nation, Israelites and Babylonians, Samaritans, Gentiles, Jews, tax collectors, and sinners, knowing our welfare is all wrapped up together, not just in heaven, but right now in our earthly cities, retribution over, rejoicing inevitable, transformative mercy extended to all. Such is the power of proximity to Jesus Christ, God with us, the kingdom of heaven, oh-so-near. This text, this truth will not only be believable, but undeniable, when we remember... and turn back... and praise God... and follow Jesus... all the way to Jerusalem and here, in the city in which we live. Amen.

---

[3] Bryan Stevenson, *Just Mercy: A Story of Justice and Redemption* (New York: Spiegel and Grau, 2014), 294.

Proper 24 / Ordinary Time 29
Luke 18:1-8

Persistent Prayer

I must begin with telling it plain: I love this parable. I likely love this parable for all the wrong, not very Christian reasons. I love this parable because the most vulnerable, least powerful person gets vindicated. The widow with no real recourse, no protection unless it is granted to her, no official status or leverage, gets justice, which could also be translated as "avenged" or even "take revenge." The long-exploited woman gets revenge. The underdog wins and this is such a rare occurrence I want to celebrate it to the fullest and high-five her and say, "You go, sis!" — maybe even wear a t-shirt that says, "And yet, she persisted." She who was likely so beaten down by the world, beats down that unethical, callous, uncaring judge through her tenacity and unwillingness to give up. How satisfying is that?

And maybe it is okay to have just a moment of shouting: "In your face!" to the system that has exploited and rendered her dependent upon the kindness of strangers. But I think Jesus' point is much bigger and less self-congratulatory than that. He tells us flat out at the beginning of this text that his point is for his followers to always pray and not lose heart, which, truth be told, does not lend itself to victory dances in the metaphorical end zones of life. The very occasion of this parable should cause us a moment or two of introspection given that it comes directly after Jesus' talk of the coming kingdom that notes that the Son of Man must suffer many things and be rejected. The last line of chapter 17 instructs those watching for God's reign to look where the vultures are gathered around the corpse. Funny, I've never seen that verse of scripture calligraphed and hung on the wall. "Where the corpse is, there the vultures will gather." Sounds

Proper 24 / Ordinary Time 29

more like a line from Hitchcock than Jesus, but there it is.

This parable today is more about our not losing heart in the face of circling vultures than running a victory lap around the sanctuary.

If we want more evidence of that, we need only keep reading in chapter 18. It is a study in contrasts with the persistent widow and the unjust judge, the tax collector, and the Pharisee and their respective assessments of themselves, the children coming to Jesus and the disciples who want to turn them away, the rich young ruler who cannot give up his wealth to follow and then another prediction from Jesus about how he must be "mocked and shamefully treated and spit upon. And after flogging him, they will kill him and on the third day he will rise." The writer of Luke added, "But they understood none of these things." Even when Jesus told us explicitly what to expect, we seem not to get it and to lose heart rather quickly as a result. We like the prosperity gospel a lot more than the one Jesus proclaimed. We want karma, not grace. We join the collective beating down of those we think need to learn a lesson instead of being merciful, forgiving, and wanting good for all.

I am right there, by the way, this election season. My default mode is not loving my enemies or praying for those who persecute the vulnerable. Maybe that's why Jesus tells this parable, given that I think only the very few consistently live that "Sermon on the Mount" sort of life. When I read this parable I want to cheer for the stalwart, eventually rewarded widow and while I may not be that callous judge, more often than not I am a self-absorbed, oblivious bystander too wrapped up in my own inconveniences to go with the widow to court and help her make her case, or do something about the systems and policies that force her to beg for justice in the first place. Does that make me any better than the judge?

Jesus told this parable to the effect that we ought to always pray and not lose heart. Notice that the "always pray" takes precedence. It seems an odd place to start in the face of suffering, rejection, injustice, pandemics, rancor, economic upheaval, wars,

The Upside Down, Backwards Life of Disciples

natural disasters, and, the list goes on.

What does this widow's persistent pleading to the unjust judge have to do with prayer? What does prayer have to do with justice? In ethics? In not losing heart? What does it have to do with us as we come toward the end of a really difficult year with the prospect of another one on the horizon? Don't we get and give a collective eye roll when someone mentions thoughts and prayers?

And yet Jesus prayed a lot, didn't he? He was praying at key moments of his life in ministry; when he was baptized, transfigured, and on the cusp of his arrest and crucifixion. Jesus went off to pray alone, he left the needy crowd and went up the mountain to pray. He talked about prayer, taught his disciples to pray, warned us not to pray for show, but instead to pray to God. The heavens opened up when Jesus prayed and he did not lose heart in the Garden of Gethsemane as he prayed, "Father, if you are willing, take this cup from me, but not my will but yours be done."

Jesus told this parable to teach us, his followers, that it is necessary at all times to pray in order to not grow weary. Without prayer we are bound to give up, give in, throw up our hands, feel sorry for the widow but do nothing to help her or change the circumstances that render her desperate. Without prayer, we may well grow not just weary but callous, high-fiving when our enemies fall from grace and commending ourselves for our own righteousness. Without prayer we lose our orientation toward God and desire not God's will, be done on earth as it is in heaven, but assume our will is divinely ordained and not subject to correction or critique. Prayer enables us to advocate for the widow and honestly hope that the judge is changed in the process. Prayer allows us to persist in working for justice and walking humbly with God and loving kindness even when it feels like a perpetual Good Friday with no resurrection in sight.

Prayer is not so much a detached, disembodied, spiritual endeavor. Rather, it is a long term, perpetual relationship with the God who opens the heavens, comes down to earth and

Proper 24 / Ordinary Time 29

relentlessly works alongside us as we seek to beat down all that thwarts the abundant life Jesus came to earth to give all people. Prayer springs from the depths of longing and comes to our consciousness, unbidden, at times when there is nothing left for us to do. We pray corporately, sometimes dutifully and daily, but I think this widow prayed so as to show up and face that uncaring, dismissive judge day after exhausting day. Perhaps that's our true and only power, too, the power that propels us into courtrooms and into city council meetings, prisons, hospitals, classrooms, and onto the streets.

It is so easy to lose heart right now. We are weary, collectively, individually. How can we not faint from time to time in the face of such inequity and suffering? But Jesus instructs us to pray without ceasing, reminding us of the end of the story, the sure and certain end of God's salvation story and therefore, ours. That is the divine *telos* of justice, reconciliation, resurrection, as well as life eternal and abundant.

The immorality of that judge was immaterial in the face of God's unchanging character. Our own limitations cannot thwart divine will, not ultimately. Some days we will relish when it is revealed that the emperor has no clothes but many, many days we will recognize that the least of these are forced to live on less and less. What do we do then? Those brief moments of seeing poetic justice on the six o'clock news cannot sustain us for the long journey of following Jesus all the way to the cross. We will only stand with those whom Jesus stands, speak truth to power, forgive seventy times seven and sing alleluia as we go down to the grave if we pray always and constantly, knowing that the Spirit translates our sighs too deep for words into a language that moves mountains and beats down the forces of evil in this world.

I remember listening to the John Lewis speak at Montreat. He said that the first time he was arrested while non-violently protesting for civil rights, he felt free. He was speaking in August of 2015, just a few months after the horrendous shooting at Mother Emmanuel Church in Charleston, South Carolina, that fateful night when those faithful Black Christians welcomed a white

The Upside Down, Backwards Life of Disciples

young man into their Bible study only to be shot by him when they bowed their heads in prayer. Just weeks after that night, Lewis admonished us to be happy because we serve a God of mercy and love and grace. He asked rhetorically, "Is it possible for us to be kind to everybody?" This man, beaten and still bearing scars from attempting to secure voting rights for African Americans in the South, still keenly aware of the racist hate alive and well in our nation, said to us, a largely white audience, "Never, ever let someone pull you down so low you hate them." He charged us, "Don't give up, don't give in, and don't give out. Keep the faith and move on continuing the story."[4]

That was 2015 and I would contend we need Lewis' charge more today than ever. But if we are going to keep the faith and continue the story all the way to the end, through to the Garden of Gethsemane and to the arrest of Jesus and brutality of the cross and the darkness of Friday and Saturday, and all the way through the confusion in the graveyard and our obliviousness on the road to Emmaus and the instruction to love not only our neighbors but our enemies, too, we must pray. We must pray without ceasing; together rather than alone. We must pray with crafted words and the ones Jesus taught us, with groans and lament and sighs that have no words, through tears and with praise until crying is no more and every tribe and nation worships together in the kingdom of heaven. Such tenacity for goodness and justice, kindness and grace, wholeness and mercy comes when we pray again and again, always and without ceasing, in words and in spirit, embodied and enacted:

Lord, your will be done, on earth, as it is in heaven. Amen.

---

[4] Jill Duffield, "Don't Give Up, Don't Give in and Don't Give Out: John Lewis Speaks at Montreat", The Presbyterian Outlook (August 22, 2015). https://pres-outlook.org/2015/08/dont-give-up-dont-give-in-and-dont-give-out-john-lewis-speaks-at-montreat/.

Proper 25 /Ordinary Time 30
Luke 18:9-14

Don't Hold Back

It was supposed to be a routine pastoral visit, you know: a pre-surgery prayer, a brief discussion about what was expected on the other side of the procedure. A: "When do they say you get to go home?" or "Will you have to do rehab?" It was questionable as to whether or not a visit was even warranted. This wasn't a church member who expected a lot of attention, a phone call that afternoon would have been sufficient, but this was a ruling elder I'd grown close to over the years so I decided to go and let her know I'd be thinking about her, fully expecting she'd be back in the pew soon and in attendance at the next session meeting.

She was one of my outspoken elders around the table. She was more evangelical than most of that flock and she talked in terms that made some buttoned up Presbyterians uncomfortable. She wasn't afraid to talk about Satan and evil and the power of prayer. She was a self-proclaimed prayer warrior who periodically came into my office to lay hands on me and pray for God's protection. If I expressed a concern, a worry, or an anxiety about anything she would declare, "You are a princess of God! Don't you forget that! You tell Satan to go back to hell where he came from!" I would nod, not fully convinced about my royal status, but glad to have her strength in my corner.

Given her support of me, I wanted to be supportive of her, so I went to the hospital for what I assumed would be a quick, typical pastoral visit.

It wasn't.

I walked in as a doctor was walking out. I walked in and saw my friend and her husband staring blankly ahead. I had walked in just after the doctor had told them that a test had revealed an

The Upside Down, Backwards Life of Disciples

inoperable, soon-to-be-fatal, flaw in one of her vital organs. Her husband shared the news with me. My friend's face contorted. At first I thought she was going to cry, but instead out her mouth came anger — at God. It was expletive filled as she railed at God's betrayal. She wailed, "Why, God? Why?"

It was not what I expected. I expected her to say, "It will be all right. God will be with me. I know God has the power to heal. My faith will see me through." I expected the confidence of the princess of God, not the breast-beating wails of one uncertain of God's care.

I was thinking she'd be more like the Pharisee, assured of God's favor, not like that tax collector, pouring out his heart to God, hoping for but not hopeful of God's response.

She held nothing back in that hospital room — nothing. Not her fear, her anger, her doubts, her dismay, and frankly, I had no idea how to respond to her honesty.

I wanted to stand far off, back out of the room, offer some spiritual platitude, or say a prayer to silence her. I was much better with the certainty of telling Satan to go back to hell where he came from. Even if the language had made me uncomfortable, the confidence in God's pleasure and our righteousness had felt good, really good.

But here was my prayer warrior, defeated. Her husband looking on, dismayed, defeated, too, looking to me for some word, any word, a word of the Lord, would have been great, a simple word of assurance or comfort wouldn't hurt.

I mumbled, "I am so sorry." Maybe I said, "I know this is a shock." Eventually, I mustered up the courage to offer a prayer. I have no idea what I said but I know I used it as an exit strategy, saying I was sure they wanted to be alone to process the news and certainly the doctor would return soon. I had no idea if they wanted to be alone. There was no indication that the doctor was coming back. I just knew after I said, "amen" I had a chance to go, and I did.

All that weeping and gnashing of teeth was hard to hear. Uncontrolled outbursts of emotion aren't common in my circles of civility and "keep calm and carry on" tradition. There are norms, rules, guidelines of behavior, even in hospital rooms and sanctuaries. Maybe the rules are needed especially in hospital rooms and sanctuaries. When was the last time someone cried out to God in anguish in this space? How many times, I wonder, have they wanted to? How many times, have you stood far off from God, from others, putting on your Sunday best and your "I'm fine" face and come into this space, your heart heavy, your soul weary, your mind anxious, your strength tapped, but your expression serene, and your prayers said as scripted. How much have you held back? The rules and regulations, the expectations and the norms, the need to appear all right, if not righteous, keeping you at bay from the Lord who longs to meet you where you are, hear your anguish, ease your burden, forgive your sins, and say, "I will give you rest"?

How much have you held back from those in the pew beside you and around the table in front of you and in the Bible study all around you? What have you left unsaid, unshared, untold, so that you can keep an arm's length from the vulnerability and fear that, at one point or another, threaten to overtake us all?

We don't have to hold back from God because God holds nothing back from us. Not even God's only Son. God runs out to meet us even while we are yet far off, smelling of the pigs, painfully aware of our unworthiness, hoarse from crying out, "Why?" or "How long?" or "What now?"

When that woman lunged at the hem of Jesus' garment, desperate for healing, decorum and expectations abandoned, Jesus felt the power go out of him. He stopped, sought her out, met her where she was, didn't scold her and say, "You should have held back." No, he says, "your faith has made you well."

When that sinful woman poured out the oil on Jesus' feet, poured out her tears, made a scene, endured the stares and the sneers of those proper, righteous people, Jesus didn't tap her on the shoulder, tell her to get herself together, offer a quick prayer, and escort her out the door. No! He said to those oh-so-together-people: This woman, she is a model of faithfulness, hospitality,

The Upside Down, Backwards Life of Disciples

and love, because she held nothing back, and Jesus, in turn, held nothing back from her.

When Zacchaeus, that chief tax collector, threw caution to the wind, didn't worry about looking foolish, and climbed a tree to catch a glimpse of Jesus, he had the dinner guest of a lifetime. The crowd said Jesus ought not be close to that sinner, but Jesus recognized a seeker, called him by name, went to his home and brought salvation with him. Zacchaeus declared he would give away half to the poor and repay people by four. Jesus held nothing back. Zacchaeus didn't either.

What have we done lately to make sure we don't miss Jesus and he doesn't miss us? When has our enthusiasm for the kingdom caused us to climb a tree, lean on our tip toes, and be on the lookout for salvation? What have we done in response to Jesus' gift of salvation? Have we been moved to sell possessions, give away half, repent in tangible ways that bring justice for others?

When have we been like that leader of the synagogue, who pleaded to Jesus on behalf of his daughter? Or the centurion who begged healing for his servant from the Jewish teacher who didn't hold back from Jew or Gentile, women or children, lepers of tax collectors?

Have we not taken *no* for an answer when someone we love is in need? When Jesus has said, "I've come for the lost sheep of Israel." Have we not held back, persisted like that widow in front of the unjust judge, and said, "Even the dogs get the crumbs that fall from the master's table?" I don't need to be a son or a daughter, even a dog will do if it means my baby gets well.

Have we poured ourselves out before the God who holds nothing back from us, not even the Son, the one who before he breathed his last, told the criminal he'd see him in paradise and made sure his mother had a son, and that the world was forgiven because we knew not what we did?

Have we been like that tax collector in prayer, begging for mercy, pleading for help, so aware of our status as sinners that we dare not look up even as we dare not shut up? Or have we held back, tried to look right and righteous, together and good, self-sufficient and aloof, far from that out of control guy beating his breast but far from God, too?

I left that hospital room, got in my car, and cried the whole drive home. I talked aloud to God and asked, "Why?" and said, "It is not fair." She's faithful and young — and she loves you, come on, God. I wondered aloud if I should have said or done something different. I lamented my inadequacy and thought hard about what I would say the next time I saw my friend, that princess of God.

I railed against God like she had in that room and I realized that maybe I should have done it there, too. It wasn't enough to say the right prayer, to dutifully visit and recite a Bible verse, to say "amen" and slink out the door. I needed to tell her, I loved her and I was dismayed, too. Now was the time to hold nothing back and trust the God who holds nothing back from us, not even the Son, the One who emptied himself for our sake, the one who pours out his Holy Spirit on sons and daughters, old and young, slave and free, the tax collectors and the sinners, the distraught princesses of God and the inadequate pastors who visit them, all of us brought close, and upheld, together, when we don't hold back from God or one another. Amen.

Proper 26 / Ordinary Time 31
Luke 19:1-10

Chief Among Sinners

Zacchaeus' parents must have had high hopes for their son. They named him Zacchaeus, after all, which means, "righteous one, pure one." A name, as it turns out, which was rather ironic because he grew up to be the chief tax collector, not just a tax collector, but that person in charge of other tax collectors, the chief among cheats who extorted the exploiters and as a result got rich. I wonder if people rolled their eyes when they saw this short man coming to get the fees, fines, and burdens imposed by Rome. Here comes that "righteous one" who stole from those who are barely getting by and preyed on the poor, that "pure one" who would stop at nothing to collect the money that goes to the state and funds our oppressor and makes him rich in the process.

No wonder the crowd grumbled at Jesus' warm response to such a notorious scoundrel. Of all the people Jesus might have called by name and visited on that day he passed through Jericho, why Zacchaeus? It seems the rich always get their way, circumvent the rules, move to the first of the line, even with this miracle-working Jesus who said he is on the side of the meek and the lost. Privilege pays then and now, the rich get richer as the poor beg at their gates and long for the crumbs from their lavish tables. Case in point: Jesus went to Zacchaeus' house.

No wonder the crowd grumbled. Just when they thought this Jesus was different, he went directly to the most lavish house in town. Isn't he the one who said he came to bring good news to the poor? Isn't this Jesus the one who touched the unclean and fed that huge, hungry crowd? I heard he said *woe to the rich* and that it *was easier for a camel to get through the eye of a needle than it*

Proper 26 / Ordinary Time 31

was for a rich person to get into heaven. But there he went, headed to Zacchaeus' luxurious house, where he ate good food while we languished here on the streets. Another sell out, we should have seen it coming. No one resists the lure of wealth and power for long... not even the one we heard say *blessed are the meek and those who hunger and thirst for righteousness will be filled.*

The crowd had followed and hoped, flooded the streets and chanted, waited and watched, reached out and grabbed the hem of his garment, leaned in and listened to his every word, yearning for justice, longing for relief, ready for this to be the day their burdens were eased and their grinding reality upended... and Jesus went to Zacchaeus' house..., that chief tax collector who got rich off of the system that oppresses the vulnerable and presses those on the margins over the edge.

Can you blame the crowd for grumbling? Wouldn't we have grumbled, too? Don't we grumble when we think God's grace misplaced or when God's judgment is lacking? Don't we grumble when God's mercy is far too, well, merciful?

But Jesus acted out of something other than popular opinion. Jesus did not strive to meet our expectations. Jesus cared neither about the grumbling of the Pharisees and scribes, nor that of the crowds. Jesus sought out the lost, no matter who they were or where they were or how that lostness was exhibited. And he responded eagerly to those who sought him out. Over and over again, when anyone showed an inkling of interest in him, Jesus turned his full attention toward them. To the leprous one who fell on his face and proclaimed, "If you choose, you can make me clean," Jesus said, "I do choose. Your faith has made you well." Jesus marveled at the faith of the centurion who came to him on behalf of his sick slave and healed the one for whom that powerful man pleaded. When the woman, that one known around town as a notorious sinner, came and poured out her tears and that costly ointment on his feet, despite his Pharisee host's disgust, Jesus welcomed her and declared her forgiven. Jesus noticed those who needed him, granted mercy to those who sought him, heard the cries of those who called on him, no matter what others thought of them. Pharisees in the dark of night, women in the crowd, lepers on the roadside, tax collectors up a tree. Jesus will not turn away from those who make the slightest turn toward him.

Jesus saw Zacchaeus seeking him and therein lies divine possibility for radical transformation. Jesus noticed Zacchaeus up in that tree and seized the opportunity for not only that chief tax collector to be changed but for the system he upheld to get upended, too.

"Get down, Zacchaeus. It is necessary for me to go to your house…now."

There is no time to waste when there is a chink in the conscience of someone entrenched in a sinful system. The crowd doesn't see it, those suffering under the weight of Rome can't yet know it, but the world is about to turn, and Jesus was about to enlist Zacchaeus to help it shift.

This was not about the rich getting richer and justice yet again denied. It was not about the vulnerable once more getting stomped on by the powerful. No! This was a glimpse into the new thing God was right now doing. This was the fulfilling of Mary's song about the high being brought low and the low being lifted up. This was how the poor's good news got proclaimed in tangible reparation. This was the Son of Man, looking out, looking up, and seeing a chance to turn an unethical insider into an unlikely advocate for every outsider struggling to survive. God, it seems, takes the chief among sinners and turns them into primary examples of life-changing grace. Those who know in the core of their being that they have been forgiven, spend their lives paying it forward, fourfold.

Jesus used our smallest urges to see him, get close to him, learn who he is to expand our view and help us see beyond ourselves and our narrow self-interests. Jesus notices our tiniest desires to do and be better; he comes to us, calls us by name, and says: let me show you a new way, the excellent way, the way, the truth, and the life. Jesus recognizes our weariness at striving for that which does not truly satisfy and offers us living water and

Proper 26 / Ordinary Time 31

the Bread of Life that never runs out. Jesus is attentive to those moments when we realize that we are exhausted from how we are living, from the suffering all around us, from the uneasiness within us, from the inequity consuming us and he says: "Come to me and I will give you rest for your souls."

It feels right now as if the world is out of control. The pandemic we thought was waning keeps resurging. Racial injustice persists with deadly consequences. The wealth gap grows, the opportunity gap expands, and the divisions between people get deeper and wider — and darned if Jesus didn't go to that wealthy traitor Zacchaeus' house while people are flooding the streets looking for change. He went into command central of this sick, unethical, oppressive system. He ate with the rich while the hurting crowd clamored outside at the gate and begged for help. You too, Jesus? But we thought you were the one to save us. We thought you were the one who cared about us. We had hoped you were the one to set us free. No wonder we grumble.

But Jesus knew something we couldn't yet see — perhaps because we are so desperate for relief. Jesus saw divine possibility, even in those people and places we thought unredeemable. Jesus saw at every miniscule turn of faith an expansive avenue to fulfill his purpose, to set the captives free and bring liberty to the oppressed. Jesus noticed a crack in the walls of power, a pinprick of light in the darkness of Zacchaeus' heart. Jesus knew that the rich, the powerful, and those benefiting from centuries of codified, systemic oppression, hard as it was for them to get through that eye of the salvation needle, Jesus knew they could yet be saved and transformed into God's instruments of justice and peace. Jesus saw the chief among sinners as seeds for a great, holy harvest that could feed the world. He saw earthly insiders and those aligned with them turned into divine advocates for those outside on the streets begging for the ability to breathe. Jesus knew the power of God to transform sinners and upend the evil structures they uphold. Jesus knew his salvation sets us all free and breaks down the walls between insiders and outsiders, bridges the divides between people, and creates not only a new

The Upside Down, Backwards Life of Disciples

heaven, but a new earth, too.

God sent the Son not to condemn the world, but to save it. Sometimes when we survey the landscape around us, we think perhaps God made the wrong choice. We think Zacchaeus and all within and around him too far gone and not worthy of Jesus' time and attention. Sometimes we may even believe this about ourselves. We certainly say it of others. But Jesus knew better. Jesus refused to give up on God's beloved world, even the ugliest, most sinful aspects of it. Jesus had the power to save and that salvation had the power to transform. That transformation brought the abundant life Jesus came to give. Even if we can't yet see it, it is coming, fourfold. Even if we cannot yet see him, Jesus sees us, knows us by name, heals us, forgives us, uses even us to upend evil and usher in the goodness and mercy that will chase us down. He even uses us to expedite the justice that will overflow into the streets, makes even us new creations in Christ... because salvation is coming... even to those of us who are chief among sinners, even to Zacchaeus because the world is about to turn and nothing, nothing in all creation, can stop the truly righteous one from fulfilling God's will on earth as it is in heaven. This very day, salvation is coming to my house and to yours, to the halls of power and the hearts of sinners... Good news is surely coming, I pray God coming through us, fourfold to the crowds in the streets desperate to know it is true. Amen.

All Saints' Day
Luke 6:20-31

For All The Saints

It is All Saints' Day today, a day on the Christian liturgical calendar that Protestants aren't exactly sure how to handle. After all, we don't pray to Saint Anthony when we've lost our keys, nor do I call upon the power of Saint Francis de Sales, patron saint of writers, before writing a sermon or article, although maybe if I had I would have gotten to the November newsletter article that didn't get written this week. I don't think our finance committee will be praying to Saint Matthew, patron saint of accountants and bankers, as they prepare the budget for the church or to Saint Christopher for safe travels, because Protestants don't believe that we need intermediaries between us and God, Jesus bridged that gap and the Holy Spirit intercedes for us, so no saints are needed. So, if we aren't going to pray to Clare of Assisi to raise the quality of cable programming because she was recently named the patron saint of television due to the fact that she had a vision of the Christmas mass on the wall of her cell the year she was too sick to attend in person, if we aren't going to do these things, then what are we to make of All Saints' Day? Why does it matter to us? What significance does it have for those of us gathered here this morning? The truth is that All Saints' Day is relevant to us. It is significant because we are surrounded by saints, not just those burned at the stake for refusing to recant their Christian beliefs, those who performed miraculous healings, or those who renounced the world in order to live aesthetic lives, but ordinary every day saints that came before us and live among us.

We are surrounded by the saints of God right here and right now, both the great cloud of them that are now in the church triumphant, but also those present here in the flesh with us. You can look around this sanctuary and see the saints of God. My friends, we are the saints of God, all of us, not because of our good deeds or unshakable faith, nor due to our pious lifestyles, but by virtue of God's saving act in Jesus Christ and our affirmation of that act when we say, Jesus is Lord, our Lord and *the* Lord. So, really, All Saints' Day, like all days, is less about us and our abilities, and so much more about God, God's power, God's mercy, God's relentless reaching out to creation, and God's ability to use us, the most ordinary, the weakest, both the meek and the courageous, to help bring about God's purposes. All Saints' Day is a day to remember and give thanks for both the saints that have come before us and the saints that surround us, but mostly, it is a day to remember and give thanks for the gift of God's equipping and empowering of people in order that God's will be done on earth as it is in heaven.

Today is a day to celebrate that God chooses us to participate in work. God reaches out to us, to you and to me, and makes us saints so that we can be caught up in God's saving purposes for the world. It is an extraordinary thought, or at least it should be. God uses not just Saint Francis of Assisi, a twelfth-century man of wealth and power who renounced his comfort and status to live among the poor, but he used Kevin, a developmentally disabled sanitation worker in Ware Shoals, South Carolina, to show forth God's love and character. Kevin's warmth and generosity of spirit to everyone on his garbage truck route, his willingness to stop, get out of his truck, go, and retrieve the trash can of those unable to roll it out the street themselves, his never failing thoughtfulness in asking about peoples' children, parents, and health, makes Kevin one of the saints for whom I will give thanks today. Kevin is surely one of the blessed by God. That is our God, the God who equips and empowers Kevin to be an unquestionable saint, daily, quietly, often unknowingly, going about the work of God's kingdom.

Today is the day we remember and give thanks to God, our God, who chose to use Saint Catherine of Genoa to be an example of humble service, a fifteenth-century woman who left a life of

All Saints' Day

luxury in order to "devote herself to the service of the hospitals, undertaking the vilest of offices with joy" — eventually even bringing her husband to penitence and the faith. Now, that's the power of God right there.[5] It is also the day to remember and give thanks to our God who chose to use Martha Williamson, a twenty-first-century woman of status who never failed to cook for church members after a family member had died or a baby had been born, a woman who insisted on helping me move when I was overwhelmed with work and small children. It was during that time that, to my horror, I discovered her on her hands and knees cleaning my bathroom when I came home on my lunch break. Her gift of hospitality and genuine care inspires me and convicts me of my lack thereof even now, over ten years later. For Martha and for our God who gave her the gifts she shares so abundantly, I will give thanks today, on All Saints' Day.

On this All Saints' Day, I will think in passing about saints like Saint Flavian of the fifth century who took a stand against heresy only to be martyred because of it. I will be grateful for his witness and courage, and I will also be reminded of the many saints I've known personally who have bravely stood up and displayed God's commitment to justice and kindness, those who have walked humbly with their God, and allowed God to make them bold to speak and act on his behalf in no less spectacular ways. I will remember Dr. John Livingston, who just this September went to the church triumphant, the man with whom I first presided at the Lord's Supper, an honorably retired minister at the time and the parish associate at the church of my first call. He took a stand in the church where he was pastor in Georgia when the Civil Rights Movement was at its height. He told his session that if they passed a motion not to allow Black people in the sanctuary, he would no longer, could no longer, be their minister. The motion failed and he stayed. Together that congregation, with God's help, took a painful look at themselves and allowed the Holy Spirit to transform their hearts and minds. I will give thanks to the God who makes saints of John and that session and that congregation and that community.

---
5   "Catholic Saints", Catholic Saints (2018). http://www.catholic-saints.info/.

The Upside Down, Backwards Life of Disciples

I will be thankful today for one of God's saints with whom I vehemently disagreed, one of the saints that fought me long and hard about something I felt strongly about, something I felt convicted was God's will for the church at that time and place. She lived across the street from the house the church had purchased for the purpose of outreach ministries. The house was going to be used for offices for non-profit agencies, for a food pantry and a soup kitchen. She wanted no part of living in proximity to it. We were at polar opposites and we were also neighbors, literal neighbors. There were countless meetings around this, much discussion that sometimes deteriorated into arguing, there were hurt feelings on both sides, but there was also prayer, and scripture reading. At the end of this process, it was decided that the building would be used as was the session's intent and she was upset by the decision. She was, to put it mildly, upset with me. Once the plan was in place we never talked about it again. But once the plan was executed and the building was in full use with people coming and going daily, something miraculous happened. At first, I noticed her taking bags of food to the pantry and then I noticed her working in the kitchen, and then I noticed her serving the guest's food, and eventually I noticed her sitting down and eating with them. That is our God. And for her and for our God that transforms her, and us, into saints, I give thanks.

Today, on this All Saints' Day, I will remember the great cloud of witnesses that have gone before us, the Mother Teresas, Saint Peters, Saint Lucys, and Saint Thomases, all the ones written about in church history books and searchable on the internet, but I will also give thanks for the ones that can't be found there. I will give thanks for my father-in-law, a deeply committed Episcopalian who came to hear me preach at Presbyterian churches even when it meant a long drive, no Eucharist and an at best questionable sermon by a not-yet-ordained, very nervous preacher. His belief that God could do something with me helped keep me on the path to ministry even when my belief in that faltered. I will thank God for choosing and equipping saints like Margaret, the elder who prayed tirelessly with and for me and whose faith in the face of a certain young death never fails to humble me and cause me to marvel at her and, even more so, at the God who was undeniably present with and for her. On this All Saints' Day I will remember people who came before me at this church because I have enjoyed the fruit of the vines that so many planted in this place. I will remember the faithfulness of the people who built this community of faith, the ones who worship with us in heaven and the ones who worship with us on earth. I will take a moment to recognize the awesome power of God to make saints of them and us in ways big and small, ways that entangle all of us in God's gracious plans for abundant life, now and forever.

On this All Saints' Day I will praise God for you, each of you, because you have allowed the power of God to work through you and I have the unspeakable blessing of being a witness to it and, sometimes, the humbling honor of participating in it. I have had people tell me that if it were not for the church and for our care and compassion, they would not have made it. I have youth tell me, by name, that some of you have borne witness to them demonstrating what it means to be people of God. I have been on the receiving end of your mercy and your Christlike love and so I thank God for the saints in this place and I thank God for the power of God's inexhaustible grace that calls and equips the saints to make it known, on earth as it is in heaven. That is our God. Let us give God thanks and praise on this All Saints' Day and every day for all those whom the Lord calls blessed. Amen.

Proper 27 / Ordinary Time 32
Luke 20:27-38

The God Of Abraham, Isaac And Jacob

"Lickety Split ice cream cones sell for $1.75 each. The Yummy Tummy sells ice cream cones for $2.15, each but will give you a free cone after you buy five. One store is offering the better deal. How much will you save if you buy six ice cream cones at that store?" Do you remember these sort of problems in your math class? Problems about various trains leaving different stations at various times, and then having to answer which one arrived where, when? Problems about oranges and bananas and buying twice as many of one and dropping half and how many were left to give to your neighbor if you'd already given a fourth to your friend? I hated those sort of problems. They were theory wrapped in practical packaging, but I always thought if I really wanted the ice cream I'd figure out if I had the money or simply count how many oranges were left after the series of unfortunate events that had befallen them and me. These problems felt like mental exercises with little real world benefit. As I read this passage from Luke today, those sort of problems came to mind.

A group of Sadducees came to Jesus and asked, "Jesus, you see, there was this woman and her husband died, leaving her childless, and her husband's brother married her, but they had no children. After this he died, this happened repeatedly — and a few more times. So... based on the law of Moses, whose wife will she be in the resurrection?" It is a theoretical question dressed up in practical garb that has absolutely no real world application. But even worse than that is the intention with which it is asked. The Sadducees don't even believe in the resurrection. They could not care less about whose wife she will be. They are asking the question to entrap Jesus, make him look foolish, and to embarrass

Proper 27 / Ordinary Time 32

him in front of the ones who've gathered day after day to hear him teach in the temple. It is an intellectual gotcha question posed by those who have the luxury of theoretical religion.

I can't help but think of the so-called "New Atheists" of our time who wrote pages and pages in order to prove that God couldn't exist. I think of the Jesus seminar scholars who gathered in a room voting with colored beads, regarding which sayings of Jesus are authentic and which are not. Red, the voter believed Jesus did say it or something very much like it. Pink, Jesus *probably* said it. Gray, Jesus didn't say it but it contained Jesus' ideas. Black, Jesus did not say it. How could they possibly really know, and what, in the end, is the point of all their debating? I think of a group of people in a particular congregation who wanted to have a theology discussion group but had no interest in talking to the homeless people who came to the church daily seeking help with food, clothing, and medical care. Theoretical, hypothetical religion is a luxury and I can say emphatically Jesus went well beyond a theoretical faith. We Christians follow Jesus, the incarnate God, Emmanuel. God with us, the one who answers the Sadducees' question with a declaration: "God is the God of Abraham, Isaac, and Jacob, the God not of the dead but of the living; for to him all of them are alive."

Our God is a God in practice, not theory. Our God is the God of Abraham, Isaac, and Jacob then, now and always. Our God, the Triune God, the incarnate God, the advocate, the stand-alongside-God, is not a "what if" or a "how about this" God. Our God is the one who calls real people like Abraham. Our God resides with real people like Abraham when they are aliens in Egypt. Our God is the God who assures a heart broken Abraham that Ishmael won't be abandoned. Our God is the God who is there when Isaac is bound on the altar. When Abraham is prepared to be faithful even if it means the death of his long awaited son, there is no room for debate, no time to speculate about one widow and seven husbands, no luxury of voting with red or black beads, no hope in disembodied spirituality. There is need only of a God in practice, a God who saves, a God who provides a ram in the thicket before it is too late. Our God is that God, the God of Abraham, Isaac, and Jacob, an incarnate God who enters the messiness of our lives and will not let us go, a God not of the dead, but of the living and all of them are alive to God because once God claims us, God never lets us go.

Whose wife will she be, Jesus? How many angels can dance on the head of a pin? If a tree falls in the forest and no one is there to hear it, does it still make a sound? The Sadducees then and now ask Jesus hypothetical, theoretical, gotcha questions. And Jesus answers with his incarnate, crucified, dead, buried, and raised life, making tangible the truth that our God is the God not of the dead but of the living and to God, through Jesus Christ they are all alive. Our God is with us when we are wandering in the wilderness, unsure of where we are going and if we are ever going to get there. Ours is the God who works through our mistakes, our lies and our deceptions, the one who never breaks covenant with us even when we are a stiff-necked and rebellious people. Ours is the God who takes what we mean for evil and uses it for good, reconciling brothers, reuniting families, granting peace where no one thought peace was possible. Our God is not a God in theory, but a God in practice. The God so invested in us and in our real world lives that God sent His only Son to become one of us, to know what it is to laugh, cry, and hurt, to love and die, and to be raised from the dead so that nothing, not even death, can separate us from the love of God any longer. Our God shows us through Jesus Christ that forgiveness isn't theoretical, it is arrested, scourged, words from the cross, tangible. Mercy isn't abstract, it is lifesaving bread from heaven, manna in the desert, living water at the well. Grace isn't out there somewhere, it is right here, as Jesus wrote in the dirt and all of our accusers put down the stones they'd just moments before been so eager to throw. No, ours is not a God of hypothetical debate, ours is the God who became flesh and dwelled among us.

A few weeks ago, our church once again participated in Second Harvest. Second Harvest is a ministry that feeds hungry people. A truck filled with leftovers from grocery stores pulled

Proper 27 / Ordinary Time 32

into the parking lot, volunteers unloaded it, bagged the groceries, and distributed it to whoever came. The thing is, you never know what is going to be on the truck. Sometimes the truck is filled with potatoes or boxes of heavy cream or more peanut butter crackers and cabbage than you could eat in a year. But this most recent delivery was a good truck. In addition to the boxes and boxes of heavy cream, there were lots of fresh meats, produce, a nice variety of canned goods, and breakfast cereal. I helped one woman to her car with two bags of groceries and as I lifted the first one from the wagon into her trunk I said, "Wow, that's pretty heavy." She said, "Must be those cans." "Yes, "I said "or maybe that frozen chicken, it's heavy, too." Her face lit up and she said, "There is chicken in that bag?" "Yes, ma'am," I said. "Oh! The Lord has blessed us today!" "Yes, ma'am," I said. "The Lord has blessed us today."

Our God is the God of Abraham, Isaac, and Jacob, Sarah, Rebekah, Leah, and Rachel, the God whose grace sometimes comes in the form of unexpected frozen chicken that will feed a hungry family. Our God is the God who shows mercy when a truck pulls into a church parking lot and siblings in Christ of different denominations, different races, different political parties, and different neighborhoods gather together to unload, pack, carry, pray, laugh, and work together. Our God is the God not of the dead, but of the living, who meets us not in theory, but in practice, the incarnate God, Emmanuel, God with us, Jesus Christ who cleanses the leper and heals the paralytic, the one who raises the widow's son and forgives the woman caught in adultery, the one who eats with sinners and blesses dirty-nosed children. The one to whom Mary pleaded, "Lord, if you had been here my brother would not have died. But even now I know that God will give you whatever you ask of him." And to Mary, who wasn't asking in theory, or hypothetically, to this grief stricken Mary, Jesus said, "I am the resurrection and the life. Those who believe in me, even though they die, will live, and everyone who lives and believes in me will never die. Do you believe this?" She said to him, "Yes, Lord, I believe that you are the Messiah, the

The Upside Down, Backwards Life of Disciples

Son of God, *the* one coming into the world." She believed not in theory, from the luxury of a distance, but in practice at the grave of her brother Lazarus who'd been dead four days. That's when we need God most and that's exactly where Jesus Christ was and is and will be, a God not in theory but in healing, weeping, forgiving, reconciling, crucified, and raised from the dead practice. The God of Abraham, Isaac, and Jacob, my God and your God and the God of our children and their children, too. God with us, yesterday, today, tomorrow, and forever. Amen.

Proper 28 / Ordinary Time 33
Luke 21:5-19

Bear Witness

What do we make of those apocalyptic texts? Those verses that tell of destruction and persecution, signs of the end times that include suffering and chaos? In this year when the word "unprecedented" peppers nearly every conversation, do these strange descriptions of pestilence and terror resonate more than they have in other chapters of our living history?

I am struck in this passage from Luke by Jesus' unwillingness to let people admire the temple. He sees them marvel at its scope and beauty and refuses to allow them to believe it will stand forever. I wonder what he would say to those of us now unable to gather in our revered and sacred spaces. Would he remind us that such spaces, lovely and important as they are to our life of faith, are not ultimate? Could this time of our diaspora be a season in which we assess what truly matters and what our role as disciples should be when the world seems to be spinning off its axis?

Throughout all these descriptors of the end times there is an inevitability, a realization of our human finitude. We do not know when such calamities will come. We cannot predict what those earth shattering events will entail. Our certain knowledge is that in life and death, we belong to God. The truth to which we cling is that when we are totally out of control, God remains fully in charge. What, then are we to do when it feels as if even the most stable and stalwart of institutions and societal norms are toppling down?

Jesus says, "This will be your opportunity to bear witness." I heard a scholar the other day note that during times of pandemic and other global tragedies, people turn to religion. He noted

The Upside Down, Backwards Life of Disciples

that such an increase in religiosity will no doubt be true in this time, too. People are looking for answers to meaning, purpose, comfort, and encouragement. People are looking for the ultimate questions of life and death, suffering and hope are in the balance. This is our opportunity to bear witness.

While we who follow Jesus cannot meet as we normally would, cannot gather in our glorious stone structures, we are nonetheless, perhaps especially now called to bear witness to the love and grace of Jesus Christ. Jesus even promised to give us the words to say when we are at a loss for how to worship and preach, teach, and serve. This time of reckoning when we see the big holes in our societal safety net, when we recognize that our rhetoric has violent consequences, when we see our vulnerability in the face of a new virus, when the injustice of centuries becomes evident time and again on our social media, calls on those of us who follow the God who came to save and usher in abundant life for all people to bear witness to these truths.

While we cannot know when these multiple scourges will come to an end or what their lasting effects will be, we do know Jesus is Lord of all, God is Alpha and Omega, and the Spirit cannot be contained, controlled, or stopped. Ours is to bear witness to the new, good things God is doing, the inbreaking of the holy even into the depths of sin and evil.

But we cannot bear witness to that which we do not ourselves see. While we swirl with the rest of society and rightfully worry about all that we cannot control but nonetheless must experience, how will we discern the signs of the times and proclaim God's Word made flesh in the midst of them?

One of the lasting images of this noteworthy year is a photo I saw of medical professionals treating a COVID-19 patient in an intensive care unit. The photo shows a team of doctors and nurses completely encased in PPE, personal protective equipment. Their eyes are visible behind shields, but the rest of their faces are obscured by masks. They are gloved and gowned. They are virtually indistinguishable from one another. Except, around their necks hang a photo, it appeared to be about 8x10 in size, laminated, a head shot of each person, smiling in their white coats. Somehow, in all the chaos and stress and urgency of caring for unprecedented numbers of really sick people suffering from an unprecedented new illness, someone remembered that revealing their particular humanity mattered. Someone heeded an insight that reminded them that we need to see each other's faces and know we are unique and valued, people with stories and families, more than patient or doctor, but individuals worthy of compassion and care.

The word became flesh and, in Eugene Peterson's translation of John 1, "moved into the neighborhood." God did not remain aloof or aloft in the heavenly realm, leaving us to our own devices or limitations. The Triune God refuses to let chaos, sin, evil, or death have the final word. When all is obscured and we are terrified and utterly vulnerable, Jesus moves into the neighborhood, the Spirit reminds us of all that he taught us, and we see the face of God in unexpected places.

This will be our opportunity to bear witness. This is our opportunity to bear witness. This is our opportunity to see and be the face of God to those fearing for their livelihoods and even their lives.

As we navigate this time that is unprecedented in our lifetime, how will we bear witness to the God of grace and compassion? How will we tend and feed Jesus' flock? How will we see Jesus in the least of these or seek out the lost? How will we reveal we are Jesus' followers through our love?

When even the temple topples and the very foundations of our common lives are shaken, will we bear witness to the God who refuses to abandon us and sends the Son, not to condemn this world, but to save it?

When everything is unsure, we can be certain that God remains faithful to the covenant and in our bearing witness to God's love, we will gain our lives. Amen.

Proper 29 / Ordinary Time 34
Luke 23:33-43

If You Are The Christ...

"*If* he is the Messiah of God, his chosen one, let him save himself. *If* you are the king of the Jews, save yourself! Are you not the Messiah? Save yourself and us!" *If* you are the Messiah, the chosen one, the king, then *show us* — so said the Roman leaders, the soldiers, and even the convicted criminal hanging beside Jesus. *If* you are the Christ, then now is the time to prove it. *If* not now, when? *If* not now, then surely you are a fraud and as defeated and powerless as you look. And the people stood by and watched as people so often do, not wanting to miss any unfolding drama no matter how gruesome. I am sure they wondered, too. I am sure they would have liked to have seen some spectacular proof that this was indeed the Christ, the Messiah, the king of the Jews, God's chosen. If you are the Messiah, then...

Is there a familiar echo to that phrase? Do you remember when Jesus last heard such a request? Remember... back before Jesus' public ministry, right after his baptism when he was filled and led by the Spirit... remember? "The devil said to him, "*If* you are the Son of God, command this stone to become a loaf of bread... *If* you are the Son of God throw yourself down from here..." Remember? And Jesus said, "It is said, 'Do not put the Lord your God to the test.'" And the devil departed from him until an opportune time (Luke 4:1-12 selected verses).

Could there be a more opportune time than this? "*If* you are the Son of God, the Messiah, the Christ, the chosen one of God, the *king* of the Jews, then show us, save yourself, do something spectacular and prove it! The people are watching, the crowds are waiting, your disciples are sneaking a look from behind corners and bushes, now is the time, turn stones to bread, dive from

Proper 29 / Ordinary Time 34

the cross and let God's angels bear you up. Give us a superhero ending to this story." Isn't it what we want? Don't you wish Jesus had flexed his muscles and summoned up his super powers and descended from the cross and let loose on those who'd tortured and mocked him? Wouldn't that be the way to show them and the curious crowd and the terrorized disciples and his grieving mother and us that he is indeed the Christ, the Messiah, the *king*?

Don't we still demand the spectacular and the super hero from Jesus? *If* you are the Christ, then stop the scourge of poverty and war; wipe out the evil people and rescue the weak; vindicate the victims and punish the perpetrators. *If* you are the Messiah, the chosen one of God, then show me a sign, turn a stone into bread, speak in a voice from on high, and give me some unambiguous direction and guidance. *If* you are the king of the Jews then take away this pain that eats me up, this hurt that will not stop, this mocking that I hear from within and without. *If* you are the Son of Man then show me, save yourself and then me and then the world will know, I will know that you are indeed the king. Like the leaders, the soldiers, the criminal, and the devil himself, we demand the spectacular as proof of a king, a king we want to define on our terms, a king we can be proud of, a winner, a superhero who makes winners of us, too.

But Jesus allowed no one but God to define his kingship. No one, not worldly leaders, not violent soldiers, not angry crowds, not sneering criminals, not well-meaning and not-so-well-meaning disciples, not the devil himself, can define Christ's kingship for him. And Jesus said of his reign, "I have come to bring good news to the poor, to proclaim release to the captives." When even John the Baptist asked, "Are you the Messiah or are we to wait for another?" Jesus said, "Tell John what you see. The blind receive their sight, the lame walk, the poor have good news brought to them." He said to James and John this greatness, "The first shall be last and the last shall be first. I am among you as one who serves." He said to the crowd that grumbles at his choice of hosts, he said of himself and of his work, "The Son of Man came to seek out and save the lost." Jesus is the King, the Messiah, the chosen one of

The Upside Down, Backwards Life of Disciples

God, the Christ who does indeed save, not himself, but the lost, the condemned, the forgotten, and the ones he touches, eats with, and dies in between. And he saves them not with the spectacular, but with what the world deems insignificant and unremarkable. He saves with the almost inaudible… "Forgive them for they know not what they do." He saves with the honoring of a simple request, not by satisfying the demand for the spectacular, but by the honoring of a simple, heart-felt request: "Remember me." He saves with the granting of forgiveness, the assurance of presence and the promise to remember the ones so often utterly forgotten. Forgiveness, remembrance, communion: These are the marks of his reign… they are so anti-climactic, so mundane, so seemingly insignificant, so very unspectacular, and yet, when they are offered by the God's chosen one and offered in his name, they have the power to find and save the lost.

Father Greg Boyle is a Catholic priest working in gang infested East Los Angeles — an area known for its poverty and its violence. He had no experience in gang ministry and what he had to offer seemed unremarkable, almost unnoticeable to most, far from spectacular.

Boyle started by getting to know members of the neighborhood's eight gangs that were shooting at each other. He found that what gang members need most is love and jobs. He visited gang members in jail after their supposed brothers had long since lost interest in them, bringing them toiletries and words of encouragement. …And when they got out, he had amassed enough clout with them to ask them to distance themselves from the gang…

For people who rarely received affection from or even knew their biological fathers, Boyle offered something powerful. Eventually Boyle's ministry led to the founding of Homeboy Industries, which finds and helps create jobs for former gang members.

Boyle's work is rooted in his Jesuit vocation and training. "We're called to be in the world what God is: loving kindness."

He tells a story of a phone call that woke him up.

Proper 29 / Ordinary Time 34

"This huge burly tattooed ex-gang member called me at 3 am," he recalled, and went on to recount the conversation:

"'We all call you Pops,' he said through sobs. 'But I need to know: am I also your son?' I said, 'I'm not your biological father, but if I were I'd be the luckiest man alive.'"[6]

Father Boyle *remembered* their birthdays. He visited them. He showed them unconditional love. He called them his sons. He had time for them. He showed them loving kindness. Forgiveness, remembrance, communion — how very unremarkable, how very small and unspectacular, how like the marks of the reign of our king, the one who came, and still comes, to seek and save the lost, the one who came, and still comes, to bring good news to the poor and set the captives free, the one who came, and still comes, to serve, the one who lived and died in the middle of the condemned and forgotten.

So perhaps instead of yearning for the spectacular, instead of hoping for a super hero, instead of demanding, "*If* you are the Son of Man, *if* you are the Messiah, *if* you are the Christ, *if* you are the chosen one of God", perhaps we should simply and humbly ask, "Jesus, remember me." Maybe then we will know that he is king because we have invited him to reign in our hearts knowing that we are forgiven, that we will never be forgotten, and that we are forever made sons and daughters with the one who came on God's terms, not to save himself, but to save others, the Messiah, the Son of Man, God's chosen one, Emmanuel, the one who was and is and is to come, Jesus, the King of the Jews, Christ our king. Amen.

---

[6] Jason Byassee, *Gangs and God: How Churches Are Reaching Out,* Christian Century, vol. 124 no. 19 (September 18, 2007), 25-27.

Thanksgiving Day
John 6:25-35

Contraband Communion

"There is someone here who wants to see a pastor." This phrase generally means, "There is someone here who needs financial assistance." It means someone needs help with rent, a bus ticket, with food, or with a utility bill. Our church policy is to not give direct assistance but to instead refer people to a local social service agency that the church supports. Many times this works, but sometimes it does not and thanks to the generosity of the congregation, when this referral does not work there is what is called the pastors' fund, out of which the pastors can help those we prayerfully discern we ought to help. I have to admit I often find it difficult to discern what I should do in these circumstances.

I am aware that I am a steward of the gifts put into this fund. I do not want to be indiscriminate. I know all about the "not a handout but a hand up" theology, the "give a person a fish or teach them how to fish" argument. I know about the whole "they might be working the system" suspicion. I have been warned that if we help one person we will be "overrun with people." I am keenly aware that we are not a social service agency. And yet, when a woman comes in my office, little child in tow, and says, "I'm about to be evicted" or "I don't have gas to get to work" or "The electricity has been cut off" it doesn't seem complicated. It feels pretty straightforward, really. All of this to say that sometimes these unexpected encounters require an energy that is not always easy to muster.

One day a few weeks ago, I was told, "There is someone here who wants to see a pastor." There had been more than the usual number of these *someones* as of late and so, when I was informed on this particular day of this person, I did not welcome the news as one might assume Jesus would. Then I was told, "He says he wants communion." There is a group eye roll. Yeah, right, he wants communion. I was thinking he was like these members of the crowd searching for Jesus for the stuff they have been filled with on the hillside a few verses prior. "You are looking for me because you have had your fill of loaves." I guess it is true, word gets around quickly after you've helped a few people. Most people, when they want to see a pastor are more straightforward, at least.

I went to the lobby and invited him to have a seat in my office. He didn't look too good. His clothes were dirty, his shirt was partially tucked in, his hair long and unkempt. I sat in the chair beside him and realized he did not smell too good either. I began the conversation with an open-ended question, "So, what's going on?" I had failed to introduce myself. In my defense it is usually the first thing that I do, but that day, for some reason, no doubt a sinful reason, I had forgotten to begin with basic manners. To be honest, I was tired, I had work to do, and I wanted to cut to the chase.

He responded to my vague question with a concrete answer, "I want to have communion." I responded with a nod of my head waiting to get to the other things he wanted, things it looked like he really needed.

Then he went on to tell me how he felt led to come to this church. He told me he was baptized here. He had had some kind of relationship with this church because he had asked for one of the previous pastors, a former associate pastor from many years ago. The man told me that he drove from across town because he wanted to have communion. He was agitated. He was mentally ill. He was afraid of the voices he hears and knows that his cats have turned against him. I began to feel for him because he was so very afraid. I wished I had one of our mental health professionals on speed dial. I wished he had gone to the counseling center next door. He needed an expertise and resources I do not possess. But part of me selfishly wished these things because I wanted to pass

The Upside Down, Backwards Life of Disciples

the buck.

But he was in my office and God had led him there. And who am I to rule that out? He knew scripture. He talked about the thief on the cross, the one who ended up in paradise that very day with Jesus and then he worried he was the other thief with the broken legs who taunted the King of kings. "But my legs aren't broken," he said, and that seemed to offer him some solace. He said again, "I want to have communion." I asked him if he had a place to live. I was still fixated on the bread that perishes. He was concerned with the bread of heaven. He told me, yes, he had a place to live. He even had a church but he came here instead. They wanted to baptize him again but he said he had already been baptized and he knew once was enough. His understanding of reformed theology was better than most.

He looked across my office and started reading from the newsprint that was posted on my walls, the ones about our congregations' core values, the core values that include the centrality of the Bible, hospitality, and mission, the ones generated as we sought to discern what God is calling us to do in the area of outreach. Somehow his reading them aloud jarred me and I apologized for having failed to introduce myself. It seemed important at this point to at least know his name and for him to know mine.

He talked more about communion, about knowing it wasn't so much about forgiveness of sin, we confess our sins before we take communion, after all. It was about being fed and sustained by God. It was about strength for the journey, for feeling close to God and supported by Christian community. He said, "I could have communion at home, by myself, but it isn't communion when you are by yourself." Finally, I got it. I can't make him well and he doesn't want from me bread that perishes. He wanted the bread of heaven and I thought I could scrounge that up somewhere in the church. I said, "All right let me go see if I can find communion elements." We will share some form of contraband communion. I would not have the sessions' approval as I am supposed to have. There were no ruling elders present as there are supposed to be. I had no idea if we even had grape juice and bread, but somehow, we were going to celebrate the Lord's Supper because it felt like someone who had come searching for Jesus at our church ought to be able to find him, even without the session's approval.

I did find our wise, parish associate in his office and asked him for permission. He said without hesitation, "Sure, go ahead." He gave me our traveling communion set and I went hunting for elements in the fellowship hall kitchen. There was about half a cup of grape juice left in a bottle in the fridge. Who knows how long it had been there, but God help us, we were going to use it. But what about bread? I searched the refrigerator. No. I scanned the counter tops and looked in the cupboards, no bread. But score! I found the shortbread cookies we used for Sunday fellowship. Why not? Seems pretty Presbyterian. I got a few cookies and headed back to my office. As reverently as possible I filled two little cups with juice that may well have turned to wine by that point. I placed two cookies on the tiny silver tray. We huddled around the coffee table. I improvised a great prayer of thanksgiving. It wasn't so great but it included thanks, praise, and a prayer for the Spirit to make that juice and that... *bread* the body of Christ. I said amen and then the words of Institution: On the night Jesus was betrayed, he took bread and after giving thanks, he broke it and said, "This is my body given for you." In the same way he took the cup and he said, "This is my blood shed for you for the forgiveness of sin. All of you drink of it. For as often as you eat this bread and drink this cup you proclaim my saving death until I come again."

The man had tears in his eyes. Through the grace of God this had somehow become holy space. I said, "These are the gifts of God for the people of God, feed on them in your heart, through faith, with thanksgiving." We each took a cookie and then a cup. I prayed a closing prayer in thanksgiving for having been lifted up through the power of the Holy Spirit into the presence of the ascended Christ. I thanked God for the gift of God's Son that sustains us. I said, "amen." My brother in Christ still had his

The Upside Down, Backwards Life of Disciples

head bowed. After a few moments, he stood, shook my hand and said, "Thank you, Jill." And he left.

I was humbled. He wanted communion. He likely still needed all kinds of other bread, bread that I know I do not have, but, that afternoon, he wanted and needed the bread of heaven and thanks be to God, Jesus had given the church some of it to share.

May we always remember that. May we remember that it is the bread of heaven, Jesus Christ, that never perishes, that sustains us, that connects us to one another and the whole communion of the saints, and that enables us to see Christ even when we are in deep need of all kinds of perishable bread. May we never forget to offer it even as we offer all kinds of other very important perishable and yet necessary bread. As we go about all the works of God may we never forget that belief in Christ is *the* work of God, the work of God that is the eternal foundation that sustains all other work, and us, forever. Amen.

www.ingramcontent.com/pod-product-compliance
Lightning Source LLC
Chambersburg PA
CBHW051714040426
42446CB00008B/877